THE BOOK OF
IRISH WIT
AND HUMOUR

Edited by
DANIEL   O'KEEFFE

The Mercier Press
Cork and Dublin

First published in 1955
Reprinted 1977, 1979, 1986, 1989
This edition 1990

ISBN   0 85342 873 5

PR
8885
. B6
1977
cop. 1

Printed by Litho Press Co., Midleton, Co. Cork.

ACKNOWLEDGMENTS

THANKS are due to the following authors and publishers who have given permission to include material in this anthology:

Mr. Niall Sheridan for 'The Action at Carrickbeg'.

Messrs. Longmans Green & Co. Ltd., for excerpt from 'Lisheen Races, Second Hand' taken from *Some Experiences of an Irish R.M.*, by E. Œ Somerville and M. Ross.

Messrs. Macmillan & Co. Ltd., and Mrs. Stephens for 'The Wonderful Thing that Happened to Billy the Music' from *The Demi-Gods* by James Stephens; 'Meehawl MacMurrachu and the Philosopher' from *The Crock of Gold* by James Stephens.

Mr. Lennox Robinson for 'Let Well Alone'.

Mr. Con O'Leary for 'Maloney on the Line' from *An Exile's Bundle*. (Andrew Melrose Ltd.).

Messrs. M. H. Gill & Son Ltd., for 'The Priestin' of Father John' from *Joe's No Saint* by J. D. Sheridan.

Messrs. The Talbot Press Ltd., for 'Meals Out-of-Doors' and 'Collars and Ties' from *My Hat Blew Off*, by J. D. Sheridan.

The Mercier Press for 'Nice Conduct', 'Rebellion of 1641', and 'Mr. Cromwell at Drogheda'.

Mr. Edward J. Delaney for 'Out of all Books'.

CONTENTS

CONTENTS

INTRODUCTION

THIS COLLECTION of Irish humour follows no particular plan and it does not seek to prove anything. Its main purpose is enjoyment. Included are some old writers, some more recent who have gone to their reward, and some contemporary writers who, we hope, will be long with us and will devote more of their time and energies to the important business of making us laugh.

Many of your favourites may not be here and this is explained by the fact that in compiling an anthology the problem is largely one of exclusion rather than inclusion. It is with reluctance that many well-known writers, both old and new, have been omitted. However, you may find here some old favourites and may make the acquaintance of some new ones.

There have been many definitions of humour from Aristotle to Max Eastman. It follows that there must be many different types of humour. The emphasis here is on Irish humour and possibly humour, like politics, has national characteristics, but the laughter which it provokes is universal.

George A. Birmingham in his *Lighter Side of Irish Life* says: 'Our own writers, while steadily denying the sentimentality, admit the rollicking for the first half of the last century. But today, nobody rollicks less than the Irishman, and according to our own writers no one is freer from those illusions which lie at the back of sentimentality.' He also states: 'Mr. Shaw is right. Nothing is more characteristic of the Irishman today than his freedom from illusion and his power of facing facts.'

This is really only a distinction between wit and humour, and Palmer writing on comedy holds: 'The witty man is rarely a man of humour. He is too keenly aware of the follies of mankind; he too easily and clearly stands apart. . . . The sense of fun in the intellectual jester—the man from Dublin or Paris—usually stops abruptly short of a sense of his own infirmity. The man of wit—

the consciously entertaining person of lively speech and quick intelligence—is usually a solemn fellow at heart. He takes the world in vain that he himself may be taken in earnest. He misses no point of the comedy but he has no part in it himself.'

Possibly Birmingham wishes to make a distinction between North and South; as too many distinctions have already been made, and as stated it is not intended to prove anything, we shall leave it there.

It is simpler and probably truer to say that no man faces facts for twenty-four hours of every day. Neither can anyone be funny all the time. It is the time a writer takes off from facing facts and devotes to humour that is important. And with Dickens' Mr. Gradgrind in mind it may even be possible to face facts and still be funny.

DANIEL O'KEEFFE, M.A.

NICE CONDUCT

By Edward J. Delaney

A RECENT small but significant addition to my library is *Courteous Conduct, or Etiquette for Every Emergency, Arranged in Alphabetical Order for Ready Reference*, by Harriet Briggs. Hence the hordes of my readers who think that my manners are no better than their own are in for a surprise, for I have turned over, not one new leaf, but every page in this most uplifting little volume.

If, one of these days, therefore, you observe me at some public banquet, leaning aside from the table with tears in my eyes and a book in my fist, you will know that I have inadvertently taken a mouthful of scalding soup, and that I am furtively searching in Section S to find out what Miss Briggs would have me do with it. She would scarcely, I think, commend the example of the learned Dr. Johnson, who in a similar plight spat the soup all over the table, and calmly observed, 'A fool would have swallowed that'.

There was, perhaps, ground for assuming that I needed a book on behaviour. There have been occasions when my manners had not that repose which stamps the cast of Vere de Vere. I never could claim, for one thing, to be an unbending critic of the convenient assumption that fingers were made before forks, and my homely way of handling the hulk of a five-pound (sterling) turkey seemed nobody's business but my own. I may even have licked my plate clean after dessert, mainly in playful mood, to rouse the ire of the Competent Authority, and mainly to get the last of the cream.

I never dressed oddly enough to be mistaken for 'county', but there may have been times, in the days before the decline of the upper middle classes, when I unfeelingly sported brown

1

boots with a morning suit, an open shirt at a hunting breakfast, or a check waistcoat at a distant relation's funeral; and never could tell, even with the aid of a French phrase book, whether I was *dernier cri* or *tout au contraire*.

Now all that is changed. I am all behind Emerson when he declares that 'manners are the happy ways of doing things', and my ambition is to have as many manners as the next. Even some of my favourite stories, which might, perhaps, be considered faintly vulgar, are off my repertoire for good, and my *Courteous Conduct* is my constant companion. It would appear from its preface that there was, unhappily, a time when there was even a greater dearth of manners in the human race, to which, as somebody said, so many of us lay claim to belong. The cave-man took what he liked when he saw it, if he was able, neglecting to leave a visiting-card in advance, or to apologise for an uninvited call; nor were there public benefactors like Harriet to beguile him into more polished ways.

The book proper begins in a practical but pleasant way, with useful hints on how to be chatty with kings, princes, dukes, marquesses, earls, counts, viscounts, barons, baronets, Colonial Governors, and their respective wives, should I run into any of these people in the bus, at a hurling match, or the pictures. It tells me, too, how to write letters to any of them with whom I might happen to strike up a closer acquaintance. I am to 'write on good-quality paper'—leaves of penny jotters ruled out—I am to 'sign the letter clearly at the end'—unless, of course, it is to be anonymous—and I am to 'stick the stamp on straight'. The language of stamps is out of fashion, and I gather that a stamp upside down on a letter to a Dowager Duchess or the wife of a Brahmin Prince will no longer convey, 'I am thinking of you always'.

Proper behaviour is not at all the simple thing people think. I knew, for example—perhaps even you did—that a gentleman raises his hat to a lady. The basic general assumption, however, that every person of the feminine persuasion is a lady, has led to many a painful impasse. Just listen to one from my Harriet: A man who meets his parlourmaid in the street is in a quandary.

The strict rules of etiquette prescribe a nod; the fact that she is of the opposite sex suggests that his hat should be lifted. Though it may be wrong, we advise him to raise his hat and not nod.'

This paragraph will probably cause you as much heart-searching as it did me. My cheeks still burn as I recall various parlourmaids of the past, to whom I most rashly nodded, in times when a nod was as good as a wink, and even upper and lower housemaids (now happy in England) to whom I may have unwittingly lifted my hat and nodded at one and the same time.

When a lady is walking with a gentleman, a genuine lady this time, not of the house or parlour variety, 'the gentleman should walk on the outside. This is a survival of the days when all roads were muddy, and passing vehicles splashed those nearest,' not, as a resourceful pupil suggested, 'so that the man could spit in the gutther'.

There is a special chapter for Delinquent Husbands, and the stern finger is pointed at men who neglect their duty. There are some, it seems, who do not confide in their wives, as Brutus refused to tell Portia how hard he found it to stick Caesar. 'The average woman,' says Harriet, thrives on affection—do not starve your wife in this direction.' There are, of course, much better ways of starving her, but even so, I am glad to report an abundance of plump and thriving women in these enlightened parts.

'When you leave your wife in the morning as you set out for business, kiss her, and mean it'—the latter part being put in to make it difficult. 'Think of your courting days, when you were spick and span going to meet her, and always be so now. A clean collar will not make up for a dirty neck even in winter.' But, thank goodness, a muffler will, even in spring. 'Tell your wife your worries, take an interest in household affairs, tell her your income, help her, when you walk out with her, to wheel the perambulator'—but let us leave this depressing section, and turn to Duties of Wives.

'Some wives,' Miss Briggs tells us, 'conceal their admiration for their husbands, forgetting that the love of a wife is the one thing which makes a husband strong.' Some ignorant husbands think there are other things which help with strength, including a few square meals at suitable intervals. However, 'make a fuss of your husband on his birthday, give him lots of sympathy, make life bright and attractive for him, do not get angry when he does, do not forbid him to smoke indoors or put his feet on the mantel, do not annoy him with tales of your household worries,' are but a few of the sensible maxims in this excellently written chapter, which gives the lie direct to the impulsive lady who declared that the best way for a woman to hold her husband is by the back of the neck.

Deportment is an important part of etiquette. 'A stride of average length should be cultivated'—do not walk as if you were stepping a patch of conacre for which you paid too much. 'Toes should be turned out when walking, but not at right angles,' anything over sixty degrees being considered beyond the permissible limit. 'It is vulgar to eat in the streets', as I could have told you myself; and foolish too. Always slip into a gateway when you buy a bun or an ice-cream, before you meet anybody with whom you will have to share it.

When you go visiting, remember that 'swearing is seldom smart, though "damned" is a good honest word at heart, meaning simply "condemned".' Do not get interested in ornaments and pictures in the room, as if you were in a museum. Do not revolve your bowler hat, poke dirt from under the carpet with your stick, cross your legs when you sit down, or tilt your chair backwards. If you do tilt it and fall, it is in doubtful taste to yell, 'Oh me hip', as if it were smashed in three places; or to inquire as if you were at home, 'What the heck is the need for all this condemned polish on this condemned floor?'

When you have visitors yourself, do not disparage the food. They will do that as they go home. Do not urge them to eat more—they will have wolfed all they can, and there will be little enough pickings for the children as it is. Never introduce a dish to your guests in the manner of Timon of Athens with 'Uncover dogs and lap'. The old Athenians were not always reliable in the matter of manners.

I would like to give you more hints from my Harriet, if I had time. Perhaps if you come round some night, I will lend her to you. I started to read a chapter one night for the boys at the local, and you would not believe how polite they became on the spot. They all agreed with Miss Briggs that—

> 'Love's perfect blossom only blows,
> Where noble manners veil defect,
> Angels can be familiar—those
> Who err, each other must respect.'

From *I Never Laugh*.

REBELLION OF 1641

By Edward J. Delaney and John M. Feehan

THIS WAS SO CALLED from being held in 1641 and other places for long after, also called the War of the Revolution from not being a proper war owing to people revoluting from one side to another. Thus, it had to be divided into four large parts, namely Old Irish, Middle Irish, New Irish, Old English, Young English, Catholics, Prodestants, Pretenders, Contenders, Extenders, Pressbetarians, Puritarians, Parliamentarians, Royalists, Loyalists, Cavileers, Roundheads, Fatheads, Sickheads, Considerates, Nonconsiderates, Nonconformists, Noncompos-mentis, Noncompoops, Regicides, Parricides, Covenanters, Recusants, Concussants, Prestons, Munros, Ormonds, etc.

MIXED

This was a mixed rebellion being partly carried out to unplant the Plantation of Ulster, also partly to let the Catholics stay Catholics, the English wanting the Deformation with exchange of wives, people with plenty of wives being soon easy to govern. The rebellion was partly carried out by Sir Phelim O'Neill, feeling his way into Ulster with pitchforks, hay-knives, razor-blades and gate-posts, also by Rory O'More in Leinster (see Cathleen Ban). This rebellion ruined all the history books, however, by being mixed, thus causing the Confabulation of Kilkenny to unmix it, namely to explain to all the people who was fighting who and for why or for what purpose.

Thus the Confabulation, wishing to carry out the rebellion properly, sent to Spain for Owen Roe O'Neill, being a great soldier, to tell him to put the four parts of the Army in rows properly. O'Neill being a good General though not English, now took an unfair advantage, putting his army between two

hills on a fine day, also dividing it into seven halves, with three
halves to fill the gaps between four halves, also a wood at his
rear, this being known as Strategy.

SUNSHINE

Munro being tired from marching, could not fight properly,
this being a good excuse. The sun was also in his eyes (sunglasses
being scarce owing to the war) this being another good excuse,
thus making Munro and his army want to go home, the English
preferring the dark, the English also always having good excuses.

But O'Neill not playing the game, told his soldiers to go
and kill a lot of the English soldiers, which they did, thus
causing a fierce battle. The English, being tired, thus lost the
battle, also Munro's wig, all because of the sun shining into
their faces out of O'Neill's rear. So was lost the Battle of
Benblurb, also Munro's wig through sunshine, not through
dark, as at Kinsale, Munro's wig remaining on the green.

FIRE

The next important thing to happen was Lord Inchaquinch,
so called from his habit of quenching fires, also being known as
Murrogh of the Turnings, from his habit of turning from side
to side. He is now also noted for lighting a pastoral fire with
people in it, in the Cathedral of Cashel, upon which ended the
people, the Cathedral, also the Rebellion of 1641, the fair land of
Ireland being reduced to a smiling black ruin, with the people
once more without legges in the ditches, sucking nettles. Thus
was ended a difficult rebellion for the student, not being held
properly, therefore not good for marks.

WART

Odliver Cromwell (pron. Corsa Crummell) was loved by all
the people, being a brewer. He was also a great Englishman
from being stern and gloomy, also from having a big Wart
upon his nose, underneath which were deep religious feelings.
This gave rise to Puritarians, who were noted for piety, being
born with a Bible in one hand and a Sore in another. They

were also known as Roundheads, from their heads always turning round, looking for somebody to butcher.

NAMES

Codliver Cromwell the Puritan leader, now being too pious for a brewer, thus turned butcher to the King; and having butchered the King, the people hailed him, crying aloud, 'Thou wart the Lord Protectus.' Thus Cromwell, by popular exclamation, became the Lord Protectus of the Commonwelt, his followers also having long and holy names, namely Praise-God-Barebones, Good-God-Squint-Eyes, Lord-God-Scratch-My-Back, Great-God-Bust-Em-All, etc., etc.

IRON

These Puritarians being pious, were now against everything, including the Cavileers, who were against nothing, being gentlemen with hair and long horses. So Cromwell getting vexed, rushed into the Rum Parliament with a naked sore and several others in his rear, shouting aloud, 'Take away them Gawbees,' upon which the Gawbees took themselves away. Thus ended the Rum Parliament, which had sat so long, a soldier named Praise-God-Barebones throwing the Maze, which was the cymbal of authority, down into the backyard. Thus Cromwell's soldiers now became known as Cromwell's Ironworks, the Maze being made of iron.

CURE

Cromwell now turned his face (with wart) towards Ireland, to bring about a better understanding between the sister nations. Ireland was also famous for cures for warts, namely a snail rubbed in to it upon a thorn, also a fasting spit rubbed in to it three times daily before breakfast. The people of Drogheda, being sorry for Cromwell gave him these cures.

CHIVALRY

Cromwell's wart, however, not being cured, by reason of his having no spit, also the snails hurrying away on seeing him coming, Cromwell was not pleased. So looking into his mirror not once but many times, he told his butchers to put their Bibles in one hand and their sores in another, also their meat saws, which they did. Then Cromwell told them to go out and butcher all the people, women and children first, Cromwell being full of Chivalry, albeit being only a farmer's son from Huntingdon, now also noted for other things. Whereupon Cromwell's Ironspikes doing as said, butchered all the people, except some nervous citizens who, taking alarm, ran away, crying 'The Lord Protectus'. Nevertheless three thousand citizens died in the odour of sanctity from Cromwell and his butchers.

No Cures

Cromwell now hearing of good cures in Wexford, namely to put a stone as big as the wart, having rubbed the wart upon it, into a bag, to be put at a crossroads, to be found by a man to take the wart. So Cromwell hurried to Wexford, the people sending messengers the length and breadth of the land to find a stone as big as Cromwell's wart, also a bag big enough to hold the stone, also a crossroads big enough to put the bag at, also a man with a nose big enough to hold the wart. This is now all well known as Folk Lower, being collected with machines out of old people nearly dead, including Songs and Shanuckles.

Bloody

The messengers having now returned, not finding nor Stone nor bag nor crossroads nor man in all the land big enough for Cromwell's wart, Cromwell, looking in his mirror not once but many times, was more displeased. Therefore he told his iron soldiers to massage the people of Wexford, women and children first. This they did with Bibles, sores, and meat saws, in a cruel and bloody massage. The children now left in Ireland were sent off to the Barbarous Islands in the West, to learn Irish.

BREECHES

Hugh Dubh now at Clonmel, 'was the stoutest enemy Cromwell's army ever met with,' many of the Roundheads being fat too. Cromwell and his soldiers coming to the wall, soon made large breeches to get in. Hugh Dubh and his brave soldiers, attacking them from all sides, drove Cromwell and his men out of their breeches, thus two thousand of Cromwell's soldiers perished, the weather being severe. Hugh and his men now being out of bullets (lead being scarce owing to the war), went off to Waterford, thus Cromwell took Clonmel, it not being a famous victory.

SEDIMENT

Ireland was now at peace, Cromwell having butchered all the people, also given their lands to his butchers for their cattle. The butchers, however, kindly said, 'To Hell with Connacht,' thus nobly refusing to take any lands, except those of Ulster, Leinster, and Munster. Whereupon the Irish people crossed the Shannon on the 25th of May, and went to Hell in Connacht. Thus was brought about the Great House, Hunt Balls, County Clubs, Demesnes, Manors, Landlords, Squireens, Shoneens, Gombeens, mud cabins, pigs in the parlour, Bedad, Bejabers, Begorrah and other well-known features of Irish life, being more Irish than the Irish themselves. This is now well-known as the Cromwellian Sediment, still in a good state of preservation.

It is not known where Cromwell went to when he died. He did not go to Connacht.

From *The Comic History of Ireland*, Part I.

MR. CROMWELL AT DROGHEDA

By Edward J. Delaney and John M. Feehan

Mr. Oliver Cromwell, the well-known liquidator, who is now touring Ireland for the first time, was the guest of honour at a banquet given for him by the Mayor and Corporation at the Town Hall, Drogheda, on Wednesday night.

The Mayor, in extending a hearty cead mile failte to Mr. Cromwell, said that the fame of his deeds had preceded him, and that his name was well-known and likely to be long remembered, not merely in Ireland, but by all liberty-loving peoples. He also apologised to Mr. Cromwell for the absence of some 3,000 citizens who had been unavoidably detained, and he sincerely hoped that Mr. Cromwell would enjoy his tour, and bring back with him many pleasant memories of his contacts with the Irish people.

Mr. Cromwell, in a felicitous speech of reply, said:—
'Mr. Mayor, Ladies and Gentlemen,

'It give me—hic—great pleasure to address you 'ere to-night in this—hic—'istoric city of Drog'eda. I am very 'appy to be amongst you—in fact—hic—your steaks and your—hic—whiskey are so good that at this—hic—moment I am 'appy to be anywhere—hic—I am just—hic—'appy —just—hic—'appy.

'Though I 'ave been but a—hic—short time in your— hic—beautiful country, I 'ave been studying your mel— hic—odious language, and I can now say—hic—"Law bree" and—hic—"Deese merra gut" as well as the—hic—best of you (*hear, hear*). Although this is my first—hic—visit, I sincerely 'ope it will not be my—hic—last. In fact, I do not feel a stranger at all, for I 'ave—hic—studied the—hic— 'istory of your—hic—'istoric land, a—hic—'istory of unceasing struggle against injustice and hoppression. I am, Ladies and Gentlemen, but a mere—hic—Henglishman, but I am, I—hic—'ope, like every true—hic—Henglishman, a lover of liberty—liberty in the—hic—widest—hic—sense of that much-abused word. You—hic—Hirish resemble us Henglish. I 'ope nobody will be offended at my—hic—saying so (*no, no*). You Hirish, I—hic—say, resemble us Henglish in your—hic—fine determination, your defiance of bad—hic— Governments, and your—hic—sympathy with hoppressed peoples the—hic—world hover (*hear, hear*).

'I am, therefore, proud to have set my foot on the—hic— soil of your storied country, 'allowed by the—hic—blood of hinnumerable martyrs. The magic of your hincomparable land has captivated my—hic—'eart; this is indeed a land worth fighting for, if one could be so—hic—brutal as to fight. I may be misunderstood—Henglishmen in Hireland sometimes are (*no, no*)—but I do not—hic—mind saying that it 'as often been to me a hoccasion of hacute distress that the moment the very—hic—name of Hireland is mentioned, many of my—hic—countrymen seem to bid hadieu to common feeling, common prudence and common sense, and to hact—hic— with the barbarity of tyrants and the fatuity of hidiots (*groans*).

'My 'eartfelt hadmiration 'as been reserved for your struggle against those who would—hic—deprive you of your hancient faith. I blush, Ladies and Gentlemen, for my—hic—country- men's be'aviour in the past—I deplore the misguided policy which would—hic—deprive you of your priceless 'eritage. Bigotry is a—hic—festering sore which heats deep into the 'eart of the body politic (*hear, hear*). My countrymen should 'ave caused several Papists—I mean Catholics, to be dissected —after death, I mean, by—hic—surgeons of either religion, and the report to be published with—hic—haccompanying plates. If the viscera and other horgans of life 'ad been found to be the same as in Puritan bodies; if the provisions of—hic—nerves, harteries, cerebrum and cerebellum 'ad been the same as we are provided with, or as the Puritans are now known to possess, then indeed they might—hic—'ave convinced my country at large

of the strong probability that the—hic—Papists—I mean
Catholics—are really 'uman creatures, hendowed with the
feelings of men and hentitled to all their rights(*prolonged applause*).

'I 'ope I 'ave said enough (*yes, yes*). I 'ope I 'ave said enough,
my Hirish friends—I 'ope I may now—hic—call you friends
(*yes, yes*) to show that I respect your—hic—religious beliefs, and
the inalien—the—hic—inalienable rights—temporal rights—of
the people of Hireland. Too long 'ave the—hic—sister nations
been separated by mis—hic—misunderstanding. The brutal
weapon of war must be outlawed. World peace must depend on
—hic—mutual charity and mutual compre'ension and therefore
I say—hic—that w'at we in Hengland desire in our relations
with this—hic—'istoric nation—the policy that we desire to see
carried out must, if it is—hic—to be—to be—to be successful,
depend in the—hic—long run on mutual good will and mutual
—hic—hunderstanding (*loud applause*).

'Everything which makes for the greatness of the Hirish
Papists—I mean people—I will—hic—support. Everything
which tends to lower the—hic—Hirish people I will oppose.
The masses must be huplifted and heducated and the—hic—the
—hic—drift from the land must—hic—be checked. There are
great possibilities—possibilities—great possibilities for—hic—
Hireland under Henglish guidance and we Henglish are always
prepared to place our—hic—ability to govern at your—hic—
disposal, so that you may in time attain to the—hic—Henglish
level of self-respect which is the henvy of the 'ole world,' (a
voice, 'Sez you!').

The interrupter having had his head removed, Mr. Cromwell
went on:—

'Justice, Ladies and Gentlemen, must be done—justice that
plays no favourites and knows no standards but the hequal
rights of the two nations concerned; and no special or separate
hinterest of one—hic—nation can be made the basis of any
settlement w'ich is not consistent with the common hinterest
of both. I thank you Mr.—hic—Mayor, Ladies and Gentlemen,
for your kind—hic—reception 'ere to-night and for your lovely
w'iskey, w'ich 'as made me very 'appy—so 'appy, kind friends,

that I—hic—'ardly know w'at I'm saying (*loud applause*). In fact I am thinking in future, my—hic—friends, of practising my —hic—profession with the—hic—Bible in one 'and and a—hic— double w'iskey in the other,' (*laughter*).

Mr. Cromwell then signed the Roll of Freemen of the City, after which he was presented with a keg of poteen, also addresses from the Town Planning Committee, the Land Settlement Committee, the Society of St. Vincent de Paul, and the Society for The Prevention of Cruelty to Anybody. In reply to these, Mr. Cromwell, who was much moved, said:

'My friends, for I now feel—hic—that I am among friends (*yes, yes*), I thank you from the—hic—bottom of my 'eart. I am in full—hic—very full agreement with the aims and hobjects of your—hic—charitable societies. I am old-fashioned enough —hic—to believe—hic—that kind 'earts are more than coroners. For, as you already know, great is charity and—hic—stronger than all things. If I may—hic—be permitted to—hic—quote from a Puritan document like the Bible (*yes, yes*). "Charity doeth the things that are just, and—hic—refraineth from all unjust and wicked things, and all men do well like of her works!" I thank you, Ladies and Gentlemen, and it—hic—gives me—hic —great pleasure to subscribe to your—hic—charitable societies my—hic—'eartiest wishes for their success.'

Mr. Cromwell then took the opportunity to apologise to the charitable societies for any extra burdens which might be thrown upon them by any thoughtless outbursts of exuberance on the part of his party, and which might have caused inconvenience to some of the citizens. As Mr. Cromwell put it, 'one cannot 'ave a homelette without someone getting 'urt,' but he assured the citizens who were still alive that such incidents would not occur again.

Mr. Cromwell and his party then left by road for Wexford where, it is understood, a reception is being prepared for them.

From *The Comic History of Ireland, Part I.*

THE WONDERFUL THING THAT HAPPENED TO BILLY THE MUSIC

By James Stephens

Billy the Music did put another pinch of tobacco into his pipe, and after drawing on it meditatively for a few minutes, he snuffed it out with his thumb and put it into his pocket. Naturally he put it in upside down, so that the tobacco might drop from the pipe, for he was no longer a saving man.

'They were surely the two men that I'm telling you about,' said he; 'and there they were standing up in front of me while I was sneezing the blood out of my nose.

' "What do you want?" said I to themselves, and all the time I was peeping here and there to see if there wasn't a bit of a stick or a crowbar maybe lying handy.

'It was the boyo in the skirt that answered me:

' "I wanted to have a look at yourself," said he.

' "Take your eye-full and go away for God's sake," said I.

' "You dirty thief!" said he to me.

' "What's that for?" said I.

' "What do you mean by getting me thrown out of heaven?" said he.

' . . . ! Well, mister honey, that was a question to worry any man, and it worried me. I couldn't think what to say to him. "Begor!" said I and I sneezed out some more of my blood.

'But the lad was stamping mad.

' "If I could blot you from the light of life without doing any hurt to myself, I'd smash you this mortal minute," said he.

' "For the love of heaven," said I, "tell me what I did to yourself, for I never did see you before this day, and I wish I didn't see you now."

15

'The bullet-headed man was standing by all the time, and he chewing tobacco.

' "Have it out with him, Cuchulain," said he. "Kill him," said he, "and send him out among the spooks."

'But the other man calmed down a bit, and he came over to me wagging the girl's skirts.

' "Listen!" said he, "I'm the Seraph Cuchulain."

' "Very good," said I.

' "I'm your Guardian Angel," said he.

' "Very good," said I.

' "I'm your Higher Self," said he, "and every rotten business you do down here does be vibrating against me up there. You never did anything in your life that wasn't rotten. You're a miser and a thief, and you got me thrown out of heaven because of the way you loved money. You seduced me when I wasn't looking. You made a thief of me, in a place where it's no fun to be a robber, and here I am wandering the dirty world on the head of your unrighteous ways. Repent, you beast," said he, and he landed me a clout on the side of the head that rolled me from one end of the barn to the other.

' "Give him another one," said the bullet-headed man, and he chewing strongly on his plug.

' "What have you got to do with it?" said I to him. "You're not my Guardian Angel, God help me!"

' "How dare you!" said the bullet-headed man. "How dare you set this honest party stealing the last threepenny-bit of a poor man?" and with that he made a clout at me.

' "What threepenny-bit are you talking about?" said I.

' "My own threepenny-bit," said he. "The only one I had. The one I dropped outside the gates of hell."

'Well, that beat me! "I don't care what you say any longer," said I, "you can talk till you're blue and I won't care what you say," and down I sat on the kennel and shed my blood.

' "You must repent of your own free will," said Cuchulain, marching to the door.

' "And you'd better hurry up, too," said the other fellow, "or I'll hammer the head off you."

'The queer thing is that I believed every word the man said. I didn't know what he was talking about, but I did know that he was talking about something that was real although it was beyond me. And there was the way he said it too, for he spoke like a bishop, with fine, shouting words that I can't remember now, and the months gone past. I took him at his word anyhow, and on the minute I began to feel a different creature, for, mind you, a man can no more go against his Guardian Angel than he can climb a tree backwards.

'As they were going out of the barn Cuchulain turned to me:

' "I'll help you to repent," said he, "for I want to get back again, and this is the way I'll help you. I'll give you money, and I'll give you piles of it."

'The two of them went off then, and I didn't venture out of the barn for half-an-hour.'

'I went into the barn next day, and what do you think I saw?'

'The floor was covered with gold pieces,' said Patsy.

Billy nodded:

'That's what I saw. I gathered them up and hid them under the kennel. There wasn't room for the lot of them, so I rolled the rest in a bit of a sack and covered them up with cabbages.

'The next day I went in and the floor was covered with gold pieces, and I swept them up and hid them under the cabbages too. The day after that, and the next day, and the day after that again it was the same story. I didn't know where to put the money. I had to leave it lying on the floor, and I hadn't as much as a dog to guard it from the robbers.'

'You had not,' said Patsy, 'and that's the truth.'

'I locked the barn; then I called up all the men; I paid them their wages, for what did I want with them any longer and I rolling in gold? I told them to get out of my sight, and I saw every man of them off the land. Then I told my wife's brother that I didn't want him in my house any longer, and I saw him off the land. Then I argued my son out of the house, and I told my wife that she could go with him if she wanted to, and then I went back to the barn.

'But, as I told you a minute ago, I was a changed man. The gold was mounting up on me, and I didn't know what to do with it. I could have rolled in it if I wanted to, and I did roll in it, but there was no fun in that.

'This was the trouble with me—I couldn't count it; it had gone beyond me; there were piles of it; there were stacks of it; it was four feet deep all over the floor, and I could no more move it than I could move a house.

'I never wanted that much money, for no man could want it: I only wanted what I could manage with my hands; and the fear of robbers was on me to that pitch that I could neither sit nor stand nor sleep.

'Every time I opened the door the place was fuller than it was the last time, and, at last, I got to hate the barn. I just couldn't stand the look of the place, and the light squinting at me from thousands and thousands of gold corners.

'It beat me at last. One day I marched into the house, and I picked up the concertina that my son bought (I was able to play it well myself), and said I to the wife:

' "I'm off."

' "Where are you off?"

' "I'm going into the world."

' "What will become of the farm?"

' "You can have it yourself," said I, and with that I stepped clean out of the house and away to the road. I didn't stop walking for two days, and I never went back from that day to this.

'I do play on the concertina before the houses, and the people give me coppers. I travel from place to place every day, and I'm as happy as a bird on a bough, for I've no worries and I worry no one.'

'What did become of the money?' said Patsy.

'I'm thinking now that it might have been fairy gold, and, if it was, nobody could touch it.'

'So,' said MacCann, 'that's the sort of boys they were?'

'That's the sort.'

'And one of them was your own Guardian Angel!'

'He said that.'

'And what was the other one?'

'I don't know, but I do think that he was a spook.'

Patsy turned to Finaun:

'Tell, me, mister, is that a true story now, or was the lad making it up?'

'It is true,' replied Finaun.

Patsy considered for a moment.

'I wonder,' said he musingly, 'who is my own Guardian Angel?'

Caeltia hastily put the pipe into his pocket.

'I am,' said he.

'Oh, bedad!'

MacCann placed his hands on his knees and laughed heartily.

'You are! and I making you drunk every second night in the little pubs!'

'You never made me drunk.'

'I did not, for you've got a hard head surely, but there's a pair of us in it, mister.'

He was silent again, then:

'I wonder who is the Guardian Angel of Eileen Ni Cooley? for he has his work cut out for him, I'm thinking.'

'I am her Guardian Angel,' said Finaun.

'Are you telling me that?'

MacCann stared at Finaun, and he lapsed again to reverie.

'Ah, well!' said he to Billy the Music, 'it was a fine story you told us, mister, and queer deeds you were mixed up in; but I'd like to meet the men that took our clothes, I would so.'

'I can tell you something more about them,' Caeltia remarked.

'So you said a while back. What is it you can tell us?'

'I can tell you the beginning of all that tale.'

'I'd like to hear it,' said Billy the Music.

'There is just a piece I will have to make up from what I heard since we came here, but the rest I can answer for because I was there at the time.'

'I remember it too,' said Art to Caeltia, 'and when you have told your story I'll tell another one.'

'Serve out the potatoes, Mary,' said MacCann, 'and then you can go on with the story. Do you think is that ass all right, alannah?'

'He's eating the grass still, but I think he may be wanting a drink.'

'He had a good drink yesterday,' said her father, and he shifted to a more comfortable position.

From *The Demi-Gods.*

MEEHAWL MacMURRACHU
AND THE PHILOSOPHER

By James Stephens

IT WAS ON ACCOUNT of his daughter that Meehawl MacMurrachu had come to visit the Philosopher. He did not know what had become of her, and the facts he had to lay before his adviser were very few.

He left the Thin Woman of Inis Magrath taking snuff under a pine tree and went into the house.

'God be with all here,' said he as he entered.

'God be with yourself, Meehawl MacMurrachu,' said the Philosopher.

'I am in great trouble this day, sir,' said Meehawl, 'and if you would give me an advice I'd be greatly beholden to you.'

'I can give you that,' replied the Philosopher.

'None better than your honour and no trouble to you either. It was a powerful advice you gave me about the washboard, and if I didn't come here to thank you before this, it was not because I didn't want to come, but that I couldn't move hand or foot by dint of the cruel rheumatism put upon me by the Leprechauns of Gort na Cloca Mora, bad cess to them for ever: twisted I was the way you'd get a squint in your eye if you only looked at me, and the pain I suffered would astonish you.'

'It would not,' said the Philosopher.

'No matter,' said Meehawl. 'What I came about was my young daughter Caitilin. Sight or light of her I haven't had for three days. My wife said first that it was the fairies had taken her, and then she said it was a travelling man that had a musical instrument she went away with, and after that she said that maybe the girl was lying dead in the butt of a ditch with her eyes wide open, and she staring broadly at the moon in the night time and the sun in the day until the crows would be finding her out.'

The Philosopher drew his chair closer to Meehawl.

'Daughters,' said he, 'have been a cause of anxiety to their parents ever since they were instituted. The flightiness of the female temperament is very evident in those who have not arrived at the years which teach how to hide faults and frailties, and, therefore, indiscretions bristle from a young girl the way branches do from a bush.'

'The person who would deny that—' said Meehawl.

'Female children, however, have the particular sanction of nature. They are produced in astonishing excess over males, and may, accordingly, be admitted as dominant to the male; but the well-proven law that the minority shall always control the majority will relieve our minds from a fear which might otherwise become intolerable.'

'It's true enough,' said Meehawl. Have you noticed, sir, that in a litter of pups——?'

'I have not,' said the Philosopher. 'Certain trades and professions, it is curious to note, tend to be perpetuated in the female line. The sovereign profession among bees and ants is always female, and publicans also descend on the distaff side. You will have noticed that every publican has three daughters of extraordinary charms. Lacking these signs we would do well to look askance at such a man's liquor, divining that in his brew there will be an undue percentage of water, for if his primogeniture is infected how shall his honesty escape?'

'It would take a wise head to answer that,' said Meehawl.

'It would not,' said the Philosopher. 'Throughout nature the female tends to polygamy.'

'If,' said Meehawl, 'that unfortunate daughter of mine is lying dead in a ditch——'

'It doesn't matter,' said the Philosopher. 'Many races have endeavoured to place some limits to this increase in females. Certain Oriental peoples have conferred the titles of divinity on crocodiles, serpents, and tigers of the jungle, and have fed these with their surplusage of daughters. In China, likewise, such sacrifices are defended as honourable and economic practices. But, broadly speaking, if daughters have to be curtailed I prefer your method of losing them rather than the religio-hysterical compromises of the Orient.'

'I give you my word, sir,' said Meehawl, 'that I don't know what you are talking about at all.'

'That,' said the Philosopher, 'may be accounted for in three ways—firstly, there is a lack of cerebral continuity: that is, faulty attention; secondly, it might be due to a local peculiarity in the conformation of the skull, or, perhaps, a superficial instead of a deep indenting of the cerebral coil; and thirdly——'

'Did you ever hear,' said Meehawl, 'of the man that had the scalp of his head blown off by a gun, and they soldered the bottom of a tin dish to the top of his skull the way you could hear his brains ticking inside of it for all the world like a Waterbury watch?'

'I did not,' said the Philosopher. 'Thirdly, it may——'

It's my daughter, Caitilin, sir,' said Meehawl humbly. 'Maybe she is lying in the butt of a ditch and the crows picking her eyes out.'

'What did she die of?' said the Philosopher.

'My wife only put it that maybe she was dead, and that maybe she was taken by the fairies, and that maybe she went away with the travelling man that had the musical instrument. She said it was a concertina, but I think myself it was a flute he had!'

'Who was this traveller?'

'I never saw him,' said Meehawl, 'but one day I went a few perches up the hill and I heard him playing—thin, squeaky music it was like you'd be blowing out of a tin whistle. I looked about for him everywhere, but not a bit of him could I see.'

'Eh?' said the Philosopher.

'I looked about——' said Meehawl.

'I know,' said the Philosopher. 'Did you happen to look at your goats?'

'I couldn't well help doing that,' said Meehawl.

'What were they doing?' said the Philosopher eagerly.

'They were pucking each other across the field, and standing on their hind legs and cutting such capers that I laughed till I had a pain in my stomach at the gait of them.'

'This is very interesting,' said the Philosopher.

'Do you tell me so?' said Meehawl.

'I do,' said the Philosopher, 'and for this reason—most of the races of the world have at one time or another——'

'It's my little daugher, Caitilin, sir,' said Meehawl.

'I'm attending to her,' the Philosopher replied.

'I thank you kindly,' returned Meehawl.

The Philosopher continued—

'Most of the races of the world have at one time or another been visited by this deity, whose title is the "Great God Pan", but there is no record of his ever having journeyed to Ireland, and, certainly within historic times, he has not set foot on these shores. He lived for a great number of years in Egypt, Persia and Greece, and although his empire is supposed to be world-wide, this universal sway has always been, and always will be, contested; but nevertheless, however sharply his empire may be curtailed, he will never be without a kingdom wherein his exercise of sovereign rights will be gladly and passionately acclaimed.'

'Is he one of the old gods, sir?' said Meehawl.

'He is,' replied the Philosopher, 'and his coming intends no good to this country. Have you any idea why he should have captured your daughter?'

'Not an idea in the world.'

'Is your daughter beautiful?'

'I couldn't tell you, because I never thought of looking at her that way. But she is a good milker, and as strong as a man. She can lift a bag of meal under her arm easier than I can; but she's a timid creature for all that.'

'Whatever the reason is I am certain that he has the girl, and I am inclined to think that he was directed to her by the Leprechauns of the Gort. You know they are at feud with you ever since their bird was killed?'

'I am not likely to forget it, and they racking me day and night with torments.'

'You may be sure,' said the Philosopher, 'that if he's anywhere at all it's at Gort na Cloca Mora he is, for, being a stranger, he wouldn't know where to go unless he was directed, and they know every hole and corner of this country-side since ancient times. I'd go up myself and have a talk with him, but it wouldn't be a bit of good, and it wouldn't be any use your going either. He has power over all grown people so that they either go and get drunk or else they fall in love with every person they meet, and commit assaults and things I wouldn't like to be telling you about. The only folk who can go near him at all are little children, because he has no power over them until they grow to the sensual age, and then he exercises lordship over them as over every-one else. I'll send my two children with a message to him to say that he isn't doing the decent thing, and that if he doesn't let the girl alone and go back to his own country we'll send for Angus Óg.'

'He'd make short work of him, I'm thinking.'

'He might surely; but he may take the girl for himself all the same.'

'Well, I'd sooner he had her than the other one, for he's one of ourselves anyhow, and the devil you know is better than the devil you don't know.'

'Angus Óg is a god,' said the Philosopher severely.

'I know that, sir,' replied Meehawl; 'it's only a way of talking I have. But how will your honour get at Angus? for I heard say that he hadn't been seen for a hundred years, except one night only when he talked to a man for half-an-hour on Kilmasheogue.'

'I'll find him, sure enough,' replied the Philosopher.

'I'll warrant you will,' replied Meehawl heartily as he stood up. 'Long life and good health to your honour,' said he as he turned away.

The Philosopher lit his pipe.

'We live as long as we are let,' said he, 'and we get the health we deserve. Your salutation embodies a reflection on death which is not philosophic. We must acquiesce in all logical progressions. The merging of opposites is completion. Life runs to death as to its goal, and we should go towards that next stage of experience either carelessly as to what must be, or with a good, honest curiosity as to what may be.'

'There's not much fun in being dead, sir,' said Meehawl.

'How do you know?' said the Philosopher.

'I know well enough,' replied Meehawl.

From *The Crock of Gold*.

MALONEY ON THE LINE

By Con O'Leary

MULRENNAN OF THE *Liberator* imagined—as who would not?—
that Maloney, the night watchman, had been born and bred
to the keeping of the door. His chest was broad for defence,
his watchman's eyes were sharp for scrutiny, his lips were
grudging, reticent lips, his cold nose smelt a rat. On sentry
go in the night, on sentry go at the outer post of activity, away
from the company, the news, the fire-places and the fun—what
a lonely occupation was Maloney's. Members of the staff pass
in or out and Maloney takes no heed. Whoever they may be
they represent to him one thing only—the right to go upstairs.
But let a stranger, an unknown, advance a yard too profanely
in that holy vestibule, and Maloney reads his design, good or
evil, in a twinkling of the ferret eyes.

It does not appear that he has thoughts, reflections or memories.
His mind seems vacant and adream even when the whole place
is agog with sensation or stunt. Let things and men take their
course—his job is to mind the door. Do not bid him 'Good
night!' (the Irish salutation at entrance)—do not wake him
from his dream. He stands amidships in that vestibule, and
Mulrennan, for one, steers past him on tiptoe. Further into the
night Maloney closes the outer door, sits in his chair, crosses
his legs, and his snores will be heard upstairs. The luxury of
that brouhaha makes the leader writers envious of that fervent
rest, and they close their leaders with a sharp smack of invective,
put on their coats, tiptoe past him, open the door, close it, and
go home.

All departments have their quarters, and at night the vestibule
is Maloney's and his alone. He does not seem to take interest
in politics or news. He cares not what the *Liberator* stands for,

27

so long as it stands for his wages on Friday night. He wears a bowler hat always, even when he brings a message in to the Editor. He is reticent. Ordinarily he seems part of the vestibule, as inanimate as it—a man with gaze instead of speculation, with snores instead of snarls, he just breathes the air. No excitement for him in the stunt, the torchlight sentence, the political invective, the rush to press, the raid, the suppression. If a civilian thumps the door you turn him away, if a soldier you admit him. There are six phrases of the door-step: 'Yes, sir'; 'No, sir'; 'What's your business here?' 'You can't come in'; 'He's busy'; 'He's out'.

But one night a little boy is downstairs awaiting his mother, who is to call for him there. When Mulrennan comes downstairs he finds his little son playing trains with Maloney. The boy is engine, train, driver, guard, ticket-collector. Maloney is passengers, railway-station, porter and station master. He takes down the whistle which is used to signal away the evening newspaper vans. He blows a stealthy note, with his fingers over the aperture to muffle the sound. He says 'Puff, puff!' 'Any more here for there?' He waves a copy of the *Liberator* as flag. He sits on a stack of 'returns' as passanger. He uses even intimate details: 'We're on a narrow gauge, sonny. . . . Allelu, the cross gates are closed. . . . The signal's agin us. . . . Pull up, there's an ould cow on the line. . . . Shunt back, the priest has missed the train.'

'You know a lot about railways, Batto,' said Mulrennan.

'And why shouldn't I?' said Maloney.

'Maybe you worked on a railway?'

'Maybe so. Maybe I was a station-master?'

'Station-*master*?'

'Station-master, I said. Master Maloney of Crowe's Cross; I was all that.'

'That's on the main line from Kingsbridge. An important station, too. And you were the master there?'

'I was and I wasn't. The big railway put up a contrivance at Crowe's Cross. But my ould station is gone to glory. The competition killed it. When I went it went, and they tore the heart out of the old line.'

'That would be the local line—the Closheen and Goonabeg Light Railway.' Mulrennan smiled as he said it, for to sophisticated people the line was a joke. To Maloney, however, it was no joke. It was verdant memory. Now he spoke freely as a man drawn to the subject that is nearest his heart.

'In all Ireland tell me is there finer landscape for the thirty miles of the permanent way? It is amply provided with stations, and I'll name them running to you now: Closheen, New Pavement, Irishtown, Ballinarea, Hollyhill, Crowe's Cross, Oldchurch, Croppy's Grave, Dropping Bridge, Shanagoshel, Two-Mile Hurdle, Goonabeg. All wan line on the main road, without ditch or boundary to impale it; no grab of farmer's land to suit the Company's design. If ever we rammed an ould heifer or an ass grazing the ditches there was compensation without litigation. Many a time I seen Tighe Linehan, the driver, pull up on the road to give an ould granny a lift. The carriages were homely and sociable—I never seen the like elsewhere. You sot all in wan line with your back against the long window, whichever way you were placed. Many the fine story and grave song you'd hear, and there would be sparring and fighting as well if you travelled from Goonabeg to Closheen after the fair.'

'It is an historic line,' said Mulrennan, as he had to say something.

'What, man?' said Maloney, with rising emotion. 'When we jumped the rails at Croppy's Grave, wasn't there a book of rhymes about it by the time all the poets and scholars of the seven parishes had a' had their say?'

'Can you recall these same rhymes?'

'Aye, and sing them.' And he sang:

The iron monster ploughs his grave and tumbles to his doom,
The passengers in merriment enjoying that leafy June,
Small reckoning ye passengers of widows they will weep
Ye to embrace the croppy boy in his everlasting sleep.
Their souls bright angels bear aloft, but the mangled bodies remain
On the treacherous iron railway foreninst the croppy's grave.

'How many lost their lives?'

'No wan at all. It was miraculous. The Canon blessed the engine at its inauguration, and Tighe was a crafty driver, never flying in the face of the Lord.'

'But the rhyme speaks of disaster?'

'Yerrah, that's the way the penny poets do be romancing. You heard tell of the dark woman of the fairies that used to be sitting on Dropping Bridge from the fall of night? Wan of the rhyming jokers captivated her with the measure of his song until she let go her hould of him and let him pass. "Your teeth are like the snow and your breast is like the dawn, your eyes outshine the glow-worm, and your step is like the faun." That was the way he got round her, and only for the fluent lie on his tongue 'tis how the ugly ould witch would have carried him off to husband her.'

'Did she ever stop the train?'

'No train ran over that bridge at night, 'cause she was sitting on the bridge.'

Mulrennan's wife appeared, and after he had seen her and the boy away he turned to go upstairs. Maloney, clinging to the reporter's sleeve, said excitedly: 'The safest railway in Ireland—'tis given up to it. A check on the tickets between every two stations. The finest station-masters—the finest body of men—and the comeliest uniforms, blue and gold like a ship's captain. They wanted to put me in a livery here, Mr. Mulrennan, a dirty black livery like crape, but I'd not demean myself that far, while I have the ould uniform sponged and camphorated all these years at home and I looking at it every day for my own company like a farmer at his crops.'

It was true that the old line vested its station-master with extraordinary pomp, though often they had to perform the duties of booking-clerk and porter as well as of station-master. By reason of the splendour of their uniforms, however, they took a higher rank than policemen, lightkeepers or coastguards. But the new line—the great company whose trains ran south from Dublin—spoiled this easeful glory. They cut into the old line's country and planted stations at Closheen, Crowe's Cross, and Goonabeg. The old line put up a feeble resistance, and Crowe's Cross was the first scalp to the proud invader. Maloney became a guard on the new line, but the old line methods betrayed him, yet fortunately not before he was known to the *Liberator* through bringing them the correspondent's envelopes from his night mail at Kingsbridge. When the new line discharged him the *Liberator* took him in.

After its one revealing outburst Maloney's spirit lapsed again into somnolence, and it took years to fan it once more to a glow. That happened when the railway stations of the new line were falling before the attacks of the Irregulars. 'Mallow in ruins! Limerick Junction will be the next to go!' And surely enough the Junction went. Now he held nightly conferences with the station messengers. 'Is Cork standing up? Any signs from Crowe's Cross?'

For Crowe's Cross he was waiting. And the night when Crowe's Cross fell, Mulrennan was hurried away to cover the job for the *Liberator*. He found that Goonabeg and Closheen had also gone. On his return Maloney met him at the door in a paroxysm of joy: 'The signal-boxes went like matchwood, I am told. The rails in upheaval. Trenches as deep as the mouth of hell. Two engines blocking the line. Crowe's Cross is finished for the new line. But the ould line, praise be to God's holy Name, the ould line is where it always was. And they'll resurrect the true cross on the ould line, and 'tisn't here I'll be at all like an ould spider in my web of misery, but at Crowe's Cross I'll be on my ould perch. I'll take charge. I'm the man in the gap. Praise be to God, I'll receive my instructions to Crowe's Cross before the week is out. God is good!'

On the following night Mulrennan, having finished his follow-up story, went downstairs. In the vestibule was Maloney, sewing a patch on his station-master's coat. Mulrennan noted the circles on the sleeve like an admiral's. On the counter lay the cap with the gold braid. He gave a cry of admiration. 'Damn fine!' he said.

'Lemme try it on before you,' said Maloney, blushing deeply. 'It's a bit narrow in the oxter and I've grown out of the breadth of the cap with the swelling and swimming of my head from the raising of my thoughts since I heard the news.'

Maloney put on the coat. For the first time Mulrennan saw him take off the bowler, and then he looked really old, for his head was as bald as a turnip. It would be an old line indeed that would have use for him now. But he put on the station-master's cap. It seemed to alter the shape of his head. He strutted up and down the vestibule with arms folded. His step was bold and free. He was not now adream. He was awake and at Crowe's Cross, and the cross gates of heaven were opened. He did not know what to do with his hands. He tried them in his pockets. Then he allowed the left one to hang by his side; with the right in turn he scratched his poll, and saluted successively like a soldier, like a priest, like a suitor; then he waved his hand aloft as if bidding a train to come on. At length his eye caught sight of the van-men's whistle hanging on its nail. He took it down and blew a shrill blast.

'Hush, you'll raise the editor,' said Mulrennan.

'I don't care if I raise the Pope,' said Maloney.

From *An Exile's Bundle*.

THE ACTION AT CARRICKBEG

By Niall Sheridan

WE WERE ALL very strong against the Treaty in Carrickbeg, and as soon as the Split came we got most of the old flying column together to make a stand for the Republic. Of course, Jacko Sullivan and a few of them went over to the Staters. But that was no great loss. Wasn't every corner-boy in the town joining up to get a tunic and a pair of army boots?

Some of our fellows occupied the barracks and the rest of us took up a strategic position in the Market House, with bags of meal piled up against the windows. Every inch of the town was under our eyes and we had a bird's eye view of Sullivan and the Staters behind a barricade at the bottom of Chapel Street.

There we were, myself and the Commandant and Tom Slattery and The Buzzer Daly and a few more of us, holding the fort and keeping an eye on the barracks, in case the Staters would make an attempt. I was in charge of the commissariat, and we had any God's quantity of bread and bacon and nearly six dozen of stout. Nothing to worry about as far as provisions were concerned. Only for The Buzzer Daly's appetite we'd have enough grub to last for a month. In all my experience I never saw man or beast with a bigger gut. Declare to God, he could eat a child with the small-pox.

Oh, he was a peculiar artist, the same Buzzer, God be good to him. Blood-poisoning from a prick of a pin that killed him in the end, after all he went through. He was never too good in the glimmers, and when it came to shooting he'd miss a mountain. But for all that he'd deafen you with a lot of blatherskite about full-sights and half-sights and God only knows what else.

33

Nothing would do him but to be a sniper. A sniper, if you don't mind!

But the Commandant said we should all pull together for the sake of the Cause, and in any case there was nothing to be gained by arguing with The Buzzer. So we dragged a table over to the window and let him lie on his belly with the old Mauser stuck out through the mealbags, like something you'd see in the pictures. Every time one of the Staters put up his head the brave Buzzer would let fly, and we'd hear Jacko Sullivan laughing the whole length of Chapel Street, as loud as a donkey on a frosty night. I needn't tell you we had Carrickbeg to ourselves while it lasted. Not a man, woman or child was to be seen.

We held our own for two days, with The Buzzer whacking away until there was hardly a pane of glass left in the town. But we were contending against superior force, d'ye see? The bloody Staters had a machine-gun unbeknownst to us and, to make matters worse, they stole a march on us after dark. Didn't Sullivan and a contingent of them sneak up the backway to the barracks? A dirty trick, of course, but war is war. All the same I thought it very shabby of Jacko.

We were taken unawares, of course, and it wasn't till the next morning that we reconnoitred the position. At first everything looked all right. But after a while I spotted someone crawling up the roof of the barracks. It was Butsy Doran, I'd know him a mile away, with a tin of petrol in his hand. Going to pour it down the chimney, no less. He was dodging along on his hands and knees, and the next time his head popped up The Buzzer let go at him and knocked the dust off the chimney about two yards away. Holy God, the crack of the bloody old Mauser nearly made me turn a somersault.

'Mother of God,' said The Buzzer, 'there must be something wrong with this rifle. I took a full sight on the bottom of his lug.'

'As far as you're concerned,' says I, like an iceberg, 'there's only one fault with that gun. It shoots where you point it.' I'm telling you that was a sarcastic one. But it was lost on him, above his head altogether.

Man alive, before we knew what was happening The Buzzer
let rip again. To my dying day I'll never understand how
he managed to hit him. But he did. Oh, as true as I'm sitting
here. I'd never believe it if I hadn't seen it with my own two
eyes. There was Butsy, falling over backwards as neat as you
like, and the petrol tin clattering down the slates into the street,
and The Buzzer looking out through the mealbags with his
mouth open.

'Poor old Butsy,' says I, just like that. 'He must have slipped
on something.' I can tell you The Buzzer took his puss out of
the window damn quick when he heard that one.

'One more word out of you,' says he, 'and I'll have the sin
of murder on my soul. Didn't you see me taking slow deliberate
aim?' Oh, very big in himself.

'It must have bounced off the chimney,' says I back to him.

Boys, but that got his dander up properly. Of course you might
as well be talking to the wall. But myself and the Commandant
humoured him for a while till he calmed down and went back
to his post.

The same day the Staters blew a hole in the wall of the barracks
and our fellows had to surrender. After that our flank was
exposed, as you might say, and we knew it was all over bar the
shouting. So the Commandant held a council of war, and
I'm damned if The Buzzer didn't get contrary again. He wouldn't
hear of a surrender. Oh, no! He was all for holding out and
making a fight to a finish, if you please. Thinking, d'ye see, that
he might bring off a few more flukes with the old Mauser. But
I told him to his face that no war could last long enough for a
thing like that to happen twice.

We discussed the military position from A to Z, with Tom
Slattery keeping an eye out of the window in case the Staters
would take advantage. In the end myself and the Commandant
decided that an honourable surrender was the only sensible
course. So he called Slattery over from the window.

'Tom,' says he–pulling out his handkerchief, 'we're sending
out the white flag. You're the very man for the job.'

'What'? says Tom, cocking his head on one side. A shade
deaf, but one of the best.

'We're surrendering,' says the Commandant. 'You're to walk over to the barracks with this handkerchief above your head. Keep it well up, or they'll think we're trying to work a quick one. Tell Sullivan we want to surrender.'

So my bold Tom starts off across the Market Square, holding the handkerchief over his head, with ourselves and the Staters watching him as if the ground was going to open and swallow him at every step. Declare to God, when he was half-way across he let an almighty sneeze out of him. A martyr to the catarrh, the poor fellow. But you'd never guess what he did next. Oh, I'll never forget it as long as I live. Wiped his nose, by God, and shoved the handkerchief into his pocket.

Of course that was the signal for Sullivan and his crew to open rapid infantry fire on our position. I was damn near being blinded for life by the clouds of meal coming out of the old bags. We were shouting for a full five minutes, with Tom Slattery lying on his belly in the middle of the Square, before Sullivan gave the 'Cease fire.' And it took us another five minutes to stop The Buzzer from blazing away at everything in sight. The blasted noise would shake the teeth in your head.

When it was all over Tom Slattery jumped up and made for the barracks at a jog-trot, waving the handkerchief for all he was worth. Jacko Sullivan met him at the door and the two of them stood there confabbing, with the rest of us watching every move. Now and again Sullivan would say something and look over towards the Market House.

'That foxy skunk,' says The Buzzer, getting a bit restless. 'He's up to some trickery or other.' As true as God, he was thinking of having a crack at him. But, as luck would have it, Sullivan went into the barracks and Tom started back across the Square.

'Well,' says the Commandant when Tom came in, 'what's the news?'

'Sullivan'll draw up his men in the Square,' says Tom. 'Then we're to march out in single file and surrender all arms and ammunition. If you agree to that you're to fire one shot within five minutes.'

The Commandant looked at his watch and gave a sort of a sigh. It was what you might call a psychological moment.

'Buzzer,' says he at last, 'you may fire one shot, but be careful not to hit anybody.'

Well, The Buzzer took up his old Mauser as if it was a lump of gold and blew the last pane of glass out of the window. Even with the humming in my ears, I could hear the Staters beyond in the barracks laughing fit to burst themselves. An unmannerly, ignorant pack, the whole damn lot of them.

Oh, but it was a comical performance to see them coming out of the barracks. Paudeen Roche in a big green overcoat down to his heels, and Mickey Reilly with a brand-new tunic and his dirty old riding-breeches, and the rest of them rigged up like a fancy dress ball. An elegant bunch and no mistake.

By this time every window in the town was crowded with people. So Mister Jacko Sullivan, if you please, begins to give a drill display! You could have heard him a mile away, shouting 'Quick March. Right Wheel. Form Fours,' and they tripping over each other at every turn. Only for I was in a flaming temper I'd have puked with the laughing. At long last, after a hell of a lot of dirty language and manoeuvring, he managed to bring them to a halt facing the Market House.

'I'll go down first,' says the Commandant. 'The rest of you wait here till I give you the signal to come out.'

I need hardly tell you we were all feeling sorry for ourselves. Of course, it went against the grain to be surrendering to a bloody bowsie like Jacko Sullivan. If he was a man of education, like you or me, it wouldn't be so bad. You know what I mean? But it may surprise you to know that we didn't give up our guns that day in Carrickbeg, nor for many a long day afterwards. Oh, no! We were just on the point of surrendering when there occurred what I might describe as an unexpected development.

Sullivan gave his militia the 'Stand at Ease' and swaggered over to shake hands with the Commandant. Doing the real big man, d'ye see. I have to laugh every time I think of it, by God. He was standing there with his chest puffed out, grinning like a monkey, until he happened to take one look

along Castle Street. All of a sudden he got as pale as a sheet.
'It couldn't be reinforcements?' says I to myself, taking a
squint out of the window. What did I see, d'ye think? Biddy
the Barge marching down the town like a duchess. It was no
damn wonder Sullivan got the wind up.

She made straight for the middle of the Square and you
could nearly cut the silence with a knife. Everyone in Carrickbeg
was holding his breath for fear of drawing attention to himself.
If she took the notion Biddy could read your seed, breed and
generation back to the Flood. On she came, like a ship in full
sail, to where the Staters were standing four-deep and every
man jack of them paralysed with funk. I needn't tell you we
were feeling a bit uneasy ourselves.

At first I thought she was going to sail past them with her
chin in the air. But that was only a bit of play-acting. When
she was right in front of them she wheeled round like a flash.

'Mother of God, will you look at them,' says she, letting a
screech out of her. 'Lo and behold the fighting men of Ireland,
the terrors of the world. When they beat the Republicans they'll
start fighting the French or the Germans or maybe the black
men of Africa. Oh, it's *God Save Ireland* we may be singing
instead of *The Soldiers' Song* from this day out.'

Glory be, but it was wonderful. The Staters standing there,
as red in the gills as a lot of turkey-cocks, with Biddy surveying
them as cool as be damned, and the populace cheering and
roaring till you'd think it was the Football Final in Croke Park.

But my bold Biddy was only getting into her stride. She gave
one look around the town and the cheering stopped like a shot.
Then she took another stroll along the ranks and fixed her eye
on Paudeen Roche. I wouldn't be got dead in a ten-acre field
with him, but as true as God I pitied him that day. You'd
think by the look of him he was going to collapse in a fainting fit.

'And who have we here?' says Biddy, examining him from
head to foot. 'Only for the coat and boots it might be little
Paudeen Roche. The Lord look down on us, but wouldn't
your poor father be the proud man to see you standing there
in a gorgeous overcoat and a pair of soldier's brogues? Him

that never had a seat to his pants nor sole to his boot, God be merciful to him. All the rags and bones he ever gathered wouldn't make an outfit the like of that.'

As soon as she stopped to draw breath the crowd gave another yell out of themselves.

'She'll go over them one by one,' says Tom Slattery to me in a whisper.

Sure enough, Biddy took a peep into the middle of them and spotted Mickey Reilly crouching down on his hunkers.

'Ah, look at him, the innocent little creature,' says she in a kind of a sing-song. 'You'd think butter wouldn't melt in his mouth. You needn't be hiding yourself Mickey Reilly, for we all know you. Didn't you steal every penny the priest collected for the Foreign Missionaries? Stand up now and give us a good look at you, if you're not dragged down by the weight of shillings and pence in your grand military pockets. Oh, it's the thieves and robbers at home we should be seeing to, instead of sending out money to convert the heathens beyond the sea.'

The cheering started again and Biddy looked around her as proud as a peacock, pretending to fix her hair, and not a rib of it astray. But she was taking in everything at the same time and I could see the eyes dancing in her head when she caught sight of Jacko Sullivan.

'Here goes for the Song of Solomon,' says I to myself, edging out on the window-sill to get a better view.

But it wasn't to be. Just as Biddy was opening her mouth the rumpus began. 'Let me out. Let me out,' roars Mickey Reilly, dropping his gun and charging through the Staters like a dog with the hydrophobia. Man alive before you could wink there was a regular stampede. And you can bet your life Mister Jacko Sullivan wasn't left at the post. He gave one look at Biddy and took to his heels at a rate of knots.

Oh, it was a grand sight entirely that day in Carrickbeg. The rifles lying there in the Square, and everyone yelling like murder, and the Staters chasing hell for leather down Chapel Street with Jacko in the middle of them, and their bloody big hobnail boots knocking sparks out of the stones.

'It's the mercy of God,' says Tom Slattery, 'that she took our side.' A simple fellow, poor Tom. But I say Amen to that remark whenever I think of my fighting days.

From *The Bell*.

COLLARS AND TIES

By John D. Sheridan

I HAVE VERY affectionate recollections of the type of collars that boys wore when I was a boy. It was as big as the tent-shaped electric-light shade that is still to be seen in the few commercial offices that are not illuminated by long rods of ghostly light. But it did not slope quite so steeply, and it might be described as a truncated cone with a V-shaped opening at the front.

In the early days it was made of celluloid, but celluloid was considered too dangerous, and a glossy, non-inflammable rubber took its place in due course. The rubber collar was good to look at, and it had several other advantages. Being firm, it kept its shape and always 'sat' properly—even when put on a neck as short as mine by fingers as awkward as mine: being deep (and you could rest your chin on it), it saved quite an amount of neck-washing. Indeed, for me, thanks to my short neck, it almost did away with neck-washing, except on Saturday nights.

But its chief merit was that it needed nothing elaborate in the way of laundering. A rub with a wet cloth put it right in the morning, and you could restore its whiteness at any time during the day—before going to your music lesson, for instance—by spitting on your handkerchief.

Like its adult relative the 'dicky'—which was a washable rubber collar with a washable rubber shirt-front attached to it—this old schoolboy collar is now completely out of fashion, except with certain sensible religious, who have kept the principle but changed the shape. Every neck looks out of linen nowadays, and there is so much washing of shirts and collars in this allegedly labour-saving age that laundry shares are soaring, and washing machines, which were once as distinctively American

41

as corn on the cob, iced water, juvenile delinquency, and tomato juice, are finding their way into the humblest European homes.

The change-over from rubber collars to cloth seems to have occurred during my last years at a secondary school, and I am sorry to say that I went with the fashion and followed the crowd. I see now that I should have stuck to rubber, and not just from loyalty, but also from prudence. For the rubber collar suited tadpole boys, and I was a tadpole boy. I would like to believe otherwise, but our family album gives me away. My Junior Grade and Middle Grade class photographs show a big head rising sullenly from a truncated cone, but my Senior Grade photograph shows a big head ligatured by a scaffold-tight soft collar.

The soft collar is obviously too small, and is just as obviously badly 'on'. Its ends are held in strangulated proximity by a pin that is on the point of buckling under the strain and is crossed but not hidden by a bootlace tie with the maker's name showing. It says much for my strength of character that in spite of this ridiculous harness I have managed to preserve for posterity the proud, intellectual look of a boy who has passed with honours. My family takes a less charitable view, and ascribes the proud, intellectual look to imminent apoplexy: which shows, once again, that there is no place like home.

(Incidentally, I have since realized that in passing with honours I made the biggest mistake of my life. For the boys who passed, not with honours, but with extreme difficulty, are all making more money than I am, and some of them are employed by boys who didn't pass at all).

My struggle with the soft collar lasted until I was well into the twenties and cast a blight over my youth and early manhood. I never attained complete mastery of the collar, and I am still a bad hand with a tie, but I moved up little by little from the low standard shown in my Senior Grade photograph.

However, it was touch and go at times. I might have joined the army and sought peace in a tunic collar, but had I done so I would have lost at one end what I gained at the other: for the privates of those days wore puttees, and whatever chance I might have had with the soft collar I would have had none at all with the puttees.

I might have joined the cavalry, since the cavalry wore leggings, but I had no horse. Besides, there was always the chance that I might be recommended for a commission, and that would mean getting back to the soft collar again. So I didn't join the army. I stayed at home and fought with my collar.

Now and again I hankered after a blue gansey and dallied with the thought of becoming a sailor. This tender day-dream got me over some very difficult periods.

I got some relief at night, when I could get out of my collar and rub embrocation into my neck, but my best rest periods were during my periodic outbreaks of boils. Fortunately I was rather subject to boils, and though my neck wasn't big enough for a really good crop I secured a reasonable rotation by eating rhubarb tart, suet pudding, and porridge, in liberal portions. When my boils were in eruption I wore a muffler and had a crick in my neck: and for a month or so after each outbreak finished I wore a muffler and simulated a crick in my neck.

Just when I was beginning to get used to the soft collar, a fresh complication was introduced, and it put me right back to the bottom of the class. Somebody invented a new sort of collar—I think he went from bad to worse afterwards and ended up by inventing the atom bomb. The new collar had four tabs instead of two, and the whole four had to be impaled on one stud. This, needless to say, was very hard on an ex-honours-student. I could rarely manage the miracle in less than ten minutes, and it took me a long time to learn to speak, breathe, and swallow, with four thicknesses of cloth pinned against my Adam's apple.

And all the time I was having trouble with my tie. No matter how I plaited the thing the knot wouldn't come right. Sometimes it was so big and loose that it slipped down and exposed my stud; sometimes it was so rosebud small that I couldn't get it off at night without help.

Two things beat me: making a neat knot, and getting the

two ends of the tie in alignment. I never got them in alignment
for years. The inside end was invariably wrong-side out, so
that I was a sort of gentleman-sandwichman, bearing on my
chest the legend Smith & Sons, Gentlemen's Outfitters. No
doubt they would have been willing to pay me a small retaining
fee had I pressed the matter, but I never had the courage to
ask for it.

However, after years of practice I learned to make a knot that
stayed in position without choking me, and to keep the maker's
name hidden on my bosom. Not only that, but I gradually
got the hang of the soft collar, and began to look forward to a
happy and only moderately-untidy old age.

But the curse has come upon me once again, and I have got it,
as of old, in the neck: for Morsel One and Morsel Two have
been given ties, and in this, as in all things else, I have been
appointed their valet and tutor. This dire calamity has come
with my grey hairs, and it presents an entirely new problem.
I have spent years learning to put on my own tie from behind,
and now I am expected to put on another person's tie from in front

And I can't do it, of course; any more than I can write from
right to left, or play *Nelly Bly* with one hand and *The Boys of
Wexford* with the other; but I daren't admit that I can't. For
there are two kinds of family ties, and in order to maintain my
hold on one of them I must pretend to some skill in the other.
My children have already discovered that I can't drive nails,
put washers on taps, mend toys, or hang wallpaper, and if they
find out that I am thumby with ties they will begin to look down
on me a year or two too soon.

At the moment I am playing for time, and fighting a losing
battle. I say 'Hold your head up' and 'Why can't you stand
steady?' and 'How do you expect me to put on your tie if you
keep squirming like an eel?' And if all else fails I say 'You'll
have to learn to put on your own tie—just like Daddy.' I say it
without a blush, though it took Daddy fifteen years.

Sociological writers and economists talk about 'white collar
workers', and I am the doyen of the corps. I have been working
with white collars ever since I was in Senior Grade. I had hoped

for a little peace in my declining years, but Morsel One and Morsel Two will have to be tied in knots for a little while yet, and Morsel Three is growing bigger every day.

In my more rebellious moments I threaten to eat apple dumpling and tapioca until I stage a second spring of boils and qualify for a muffler, and sometimes I promise myself that when I retire I'll take a cottage by the sea, grow a beard, and lay in a stock of blue gansies. But I am a little bit late now to be planning desperate remedies, and it seems that, for better for worse, I am tied to the collar.

From *My Hat Blew Off*.

MEALS OUT-OF-DOORS

By *John D. Sheridan*

I AM ALL FOR EATING out-of-doors when the alternative is to go hungry; and in this I am supported by the unrecorded opinions of hedge-trimmers, turf-cutters, hay-makers, road-menders, infantrymen, and other knowledgeable people. For those who, for professional reasons, are sometimes forced to feed in the open, are always glad to have four walls about them when they take their meat, and if they have any choice in the matter they will plump for a roof.

By a strange confusion of thought, many people think that a meal out-of-doors is a magnificent thing, where as the truth is that a meal is so magnificent a thing that it can be enjoyed anywhere—even out-of-doors. But—and make no mistake about it—the enjoyment is in proportion to the amount of shelter provided. Fresh air may add something to the appetite, but it always takes something from the meal. The sensible thing is, not to take the meal out with you, but to take the appetite home with you. When you eat in the open air there is nothing between you and the North Pole, so that you share your meal with the whole world. You have no more privacy than a cow, and not nearly as much comfort.

Country folk, with centuries of true culture behind them, never take their food out-of-doors—unless some desperate adventure is afoot, like mowing the far meadow, or selling a cow in the neighbouring town. They may bring a can of tea to the meadow, or a few monster sandwiches to the town, but when they do they have the air of exiles, and they are always glad to get back again to the one place where a human being can eat properly. They honour a tradition that dates from the time when men first began to cook their food and to use

implements to divide it up with—the tradition of the table.
For the table is the first priority of civilized living, and the
oldest and most necessary of our household pieces. It is a sacred
thing, and not even the Law may lay hands on it; the bailiff is
free to seize your piano, but he must leave you your table.

With a table, and a rug on the floor, you can set up house.
You may sleep on the floor if you will, but to eat off it is barbarism,
and to pick your food off the ground is worse still. Every time
you go on a picnic you sell your birthright and become a beast
of the field.

A mild form of the picnic habit is that sin of the suburbs
—tea in the garden. This is a perversion that has nothing to
recommend it. It involves fuss and discomfort, long waits for
milk and sugar, and surreptitious juggling feats with sodden
pieces of cake, jittery knees, and buttery fingers. It makes you
the sport of crawlers and flying things, gives you the company
of ants, earwigs, wasps, beetles, and buzz-flies, and leaves
you with no hand free to discourage the dog from next door.
You are always either a little too hot or a little too cold, and
though you seldom get enough to eat you get enough to cheat
you out of a meal afterwards.

Tea on the beach is much worse than tea in the garden—the
difference between them is much the same as the difference
between manslaughter due to a sudden whim, and cold, pre-
meditated murder. Tea on the beach might be more excusable,
and more bearable, if the other members of the party regarded
it as a meal under difficulties, and did not try to act as if the
difficulties were the best part of the meal. But the fanatical
picnicker has no sense of his dignity (though it is usually her
dignity) as a human being. She gets down on her knees to puff
life into a fire of twigs, takes your sports coat to shield the flame,
and sends you to borrow a kettle of water from decent cottage
folk who, very properly, look on you as a confounded nuisance,
and a cracked one at that.

The real crux of the picnic is the milk. When each of the
company has a cup of black tea in his hand, and is afraid to

move, in spite of the cramp in his leg, lest he be scalded to death, or should overturn the primus, the chief steward says 'The Milk!' And we all know what she means. There is no milk. So you honour the toast of absent friends and wait for the tea to become cool enough for drinking.

Once in a while, the milk is not left at home, and on these rare occasions it turns sour (in sympathy with the rest of us), or is tumbled by one of the children, or sheds its cork in the bottom of a haver-sack. So that, one way or another, there is never enough milk.

Not that it matters very much. For human beings, since they eat with their hands, and have only two hands apiece, are not properly equipped for eating in the open; they can't take bite and sup alternately in the good old time-honoured way, but must eat whole sandwiches at a time between acrobatic gulps of tea. And there are other little miseries. For one thing, most of the sandwiches are almost completely blind, and the bottom of every paper bag is an inch deep in tomato fragments, white of egg, and gobbets of ham. For another, the tea tastes of smoke, or paraffin, or both. Your mouth is gritty with sand, and when a fly lands on your nose you can do nothing but stick out your lower lip and try to blow him off.

All this could be borne were it not for the rude shouts that go with it, for the sufferers encourage each other with cries of 'Isn't it lovely?' and 'There's nothing like a meal in the open!' They fight amongst themselves for the honour of refusing the last soggy sandwich, and shake their heads to indicate that they are replete. Meanwhile, hidden in the bent grass, long-tailed field mice are sniffing anxiously and wondering if they will get their own picnic finished before the rats and seagulls arrive to dispose of the litter.

The Americans are very fond of picnics, and they call them by such fancy names as clambakes and barbecues. But their technique is vastly different from ours. In the first place, they go picknicking, not in fives and sixes, but in hundreds, and they roast an ox where we should simply go down to the grocer for a pound of cooked ham. And instead of having a meal far away and putting up with the discomforts, they eat in the nearest meadow and avoid most of the discomforts.

I was at one American picnic, and it was held in a secluded dell about four hundred yards from a big country mansion: and the mansion, in its turn, was about nine hundred yards from the outskirts of a growing town. An enormous brick oven was set up in the secluded dell, and over it two professional chefs, in white caps, and with the aid of fourteen assistants, toasted and grilled enough meat for a regiment. The whole setting was primitive in the extreme.

We sat at long wooden tables covered with freshly-laundered white cloths, and we had a serviette apiece. We sat there, yards and yards from civilization, and watched the chipmunks play in the pines over our heads. And between courses you could run back to the house for your cigarettes.

Nor was the menu very elaborate. After all, picnickers cannot expect to feed like princes, so we had to be content with grilled trout, steak and mushrooms, turkey sandwiches, corn-on-the-cob, roast pork, ice cream, melons, peaches, grapes, trifle, coffee, and soft drinks. And after the meal, a gentleman in a ten-gallon hat sang us cowboy songs and accompanied himself on a hilly-billy banjo. He fitted in perfectly with the rude, rural surroundings, and we should have liked to hear more of him, but he was appearing by kind permission of the neighbouring radio station, and after he sang five or six songs he had to hurry back to a rehearsal.

It was all very simple, very rustic, and very enjoyable. After the rush and bustle of city life it was pleasant indeed to sit there, deep in the heart of the woods, watching the chefs and the chipmunks, eating plain, simple food, and living the life that the hardy pioneers lived when they trekked cross the prairies in their trundling waggons. It was a moment that I shall always remember, and if I ever forget, all I have to do is to look at the flashlight photographs that the pressmen took.

For me, there were only two flaws in the proceedings. The first was that they were held in the open air. The second was that when I got back to the big country mansion, I wanted to eat (I always want to eat after a few hours in the open air), and I hadn't the heart to ask for my supper.

From *My Hat Blew Off*.

DANIEL O'CONNELL AND BIDDY MORIARTY

'WHAT'S THE PRICE of this walking-stick, Mrs. What's-your-name?'

'Moriarty, sir, is my name, and a good one it is; and what have you to say agin it? and one and sixpence is the price of this stick—troth 'tis chape as dirt—so it is.'

'One and sixpence for a walking-stick! Whew! Why you are no better than an impostor to ask eighteenpence for what cost you twopence.'

'Twopence, your grandmother,' replied Biddy. 'Do you mane to say it is cheating the people I am? Impostor indeed!'

'Ay, impostor; and it's that I call you to your teeth,' rejoined O'Connell.

'Come, cut your stick, you cantankerous jackanapes.'

'Keep a civil tongue in your head, you old diagonal!' cried O'Connell calmly.

'Stop your jaw, you pug-nosed badger, or by this and that,' cried Mrs. Moriarty, 'I'll make you go quicker than you came.'

'Don't be in a passion, my old radius; anger will only wrinkle your beauty.'

'By the holy, if you say another word of impudence, I'll tan your dirty hide, you bastely scrub; and sorry I'd be to soil my fists upon your carcase.'

'Whew, boys, what a passion Old Biddy is in! I protest, as I'm a gentleman.'

'Gintleman! gintleman! the likes of you a gintleman! Wisha that bangs Banagher. Why, you potato-faced pippin-squeezer, where did a Madagascar monkey like you pick up enough of common Christian dacency to hide your Kerry brogue?'

'Easy now, easy now,' cried O'Connell, with imperturbable good-humour, 'don't choke yourself with fine language, you old whiskey-drinking parallelogram.'

'What's that you call me, you murdering villain?' roared Mrs. Moriarty, stung with fury.

'I call you,' answered O'Connell, 'a parallelogram, and a Dublin judge and jury will say it's no libel to call you so.'

'Oh tare and ounds! oh, you ruffin! that an honest woman like me should be called parrybellygrum to her face. I'm none of your parrybellygrums, you rascally gallows-bird; you cowardly, sneaking, plate-licken blaggard.'

'Oh, not you, indeed,' retorted O'Connell. 'Why, I suppose you deny that you keep a hypothenuse in your house.'

'It's a lie for you, you robber: I never had such a thing in my house, you swindling thief.'

'Ah, you can't deny the charge, you miserable sub-multiple of a duplicate ratio.'

'You saucy tinker's apprentice, if you don't cease you jaw, I'll——' But here she gasped for breath, while O'Connell proceeded——

'While I have a tongue I'll abuse you, you most inimitable periphery. Look at her, boys; there she stands a convicted perpendicular in petticoats! There she trembles with guilt down to the extremities of her corollaries. Ah! your'e found out, you rectilineal antecedent, and equiangular old hag; you porter-swiping similitude of the bisection of a vortex.'

Overwhelmed with this torrent of language, Mrs. Moriarty was silenced. Catching up a saucepan, she was aiming at O'Connell's head, when he prudently made a timely retreat.

DORIAN GRAY

By Oscar Wilde

IT WAS TEA-TIME, and the mellow light of the huge lace-covered lamp that stood on the table lit up the delicate china and hammered silver of the service at which the Duchess was presiding. Her white hands were moving daintily among the cups, and her full red lips were smiling at something that Dorian had whispered to her. Lord Henry was lying back in a silk-draped wicker-chair looking at them. On a peach-coloured divan sat Lady Narborough pretending to listen to the Duke's description of the last Brazilian beetle that he had added to his collection. Three young men in elaborate smoking-suits were handing tea-cakes to some of the women. The house-party consisted of twelve people, and there were more expected to arrive on the next day.

'What are you two talking about?' said Lord Henry, strolling over to the table, and putting his cup down. 'I hope Dorian has told you about my plans for re-christening everything, Gladys. It is a delightful idea.'

'But I don't want to be re-christened, Harry,' rejoined the Duchess, looking up at him with her wonderful eyes. 'I am quite satisfied with my own name, and I am sure Mr. Gray should be satisfied with his.'

'My dear Gladys, I would not alter either name for the world. They are both perfect. I was thinking chiefly of flowers. Yesterday I cut an orchid, for my buttonhole. It was a marvellous spotted thing, as effective as the seven deadly sins. In a thoughtless moment I asked one of the gardeners what it was called. He told me it was a fine specimen of *Robinsoniana*, or something dreadful of that kind. It is a sad truth, but we have lost the faculty of giving lovely names to things. Names are everything.

I never quarrel with actions. My one quarrel is with words. That is the reason I hate vulgar realism in literature. The man who could call a spade a spade should be compelled to use one. It is the only thing he is fit for.'

'Then what should we call you, Harry?' she asked.

'His name is Prince Paradox,' said Dorian.

'I recognize him in a flash,' exclaimed the Duchess.

'I won't hear of it,' laughed Lord Henry, sinking into a chair. 'From a label there is no escape! I refuse the title.'

'Royalties may not abdicate,' fell as a warning from pretty lips.

'You wish me to defend my throne, then?'

'Yes.'

'I give the truths of tomorrow.'

'I prefer the mistakes of today,' she answered.

'You disarm me, Gladys,' he cried, catching the wilfulness of her mood.

'Of your shield, Harry: not of your spear.'

'I never tilt against beauty,' he said, with a wave of his hand.

'That is your error, Harry, believe me. You value beauty far too much.'

'How can you say that? I admit that I think that it is better to be beautiful than to be good. But on the other hand no one is more ready than I am to acknowledge that it is better to be good than to be ugly.'

'Ugliness is one of the seven deadly sins, then?' cried the Duchess. 'What becomes of your simile about the orchid?'

'Ugliness is one of the seven deadly virtues, Gladys. You, as a good Tory, must not underrate them. Beer, the Bible, and the seven deadly virtues have made our England what she is.'

'You don't like your country, then?' she asked.

'I live in it.'

'That you may censure it the better.'

'Would you have me take the verdict of Europe on it?' he inquired.

'What do they say of us?'

'That Tartuffe has emigrated to England and opened a shop.'

'Is that yours, Harry?'

'I give it to you.'

'I could not use it. It is too true.'

'You need not be afraid. Our countrymen never recognize a description.'

'They are practical.'

'They are more cunning than practical. When they make up their ledger, they balance stupidity by wealth, and vice by hypocrisy.'

'Still, we have done great things.'

'Great things have been thrust on us, Gladys.'

'We have carried their burden.'

'Only as far as the Stock Exchange.'

She shook her head. 'I believe in the race,' she cried.

'It represents the survival of the pushing.'

'It has development.'

'Decay fascinates me more.'

'What of Art?' she asked.

'It is a malady.'

'Love?'

'An illusion.'

'Religion?'

'The fashionable substitute for Belief.'

'You are a sceptic.'

'Never! Scepticism is the beginning of Faith.'

'What are you?'

'To define is to limit.'

'Give me a clue.'

'Threads snap. You would lose your way in the labyrinth.'

'You bewilder me. Let us talk of some one else.'

'Our host is a delightful topic. Years ago he was christened Prince Charming.'

'Ah! don't remind me of that,' cried Dorian Gray.

'Our host is rather horrid this evening,' answered the Duchess, colouring. 'I believe he thinks that Monmouth married me on purely scientific principles as the best specimen he could find of a modern butterfly.'

'Well, I hope he won't stick pins into you, Duchess,' laughed Dorian.

'Oh! my maid does that already, Mr. Gray, when she is annoyed with me.'

'And what does she get annoyed with you about, Duchess?'

'For the most trivial things, Mr. Gray, I assure you. Usually because I come in at ten minutes to nine and tell her that I must be dressed by half-past eight.'

'How unreasonable of her! You should give her warning.'

'I daren't, Mr. Gray. Why, she invents hats for me. You remember the one I wore at Lady Hillstone's garden-party? You don't, but it is nice of you to pretend that you do. Well, she made it out of nothing. All good hats are made out of nothing.'

'Like all good reputations, Gladys,' interrupted Lord Henry. 'Every effect that one produces gives one an enemy. To be popular one must be a mediocrity.'

'Not with women,' said the Duchess, shaking her head; 'and women rule the world. I assure you we can't bear mediocrities. We women, as some one says, love with our ears, just as you men love with your eyes, if you ever love at all.'

'It seems to me that we never do anything else,' murmured Dorian.

'Ah! then, you never really love, Mr. Gray,' answered the Duchess, with mock sadness.

'My dear Gladys!' cried Lord Henry. 'How can you say that? Romance lives by repetition, and repetition converts an appetite into an art. Besides, each time that one loves is the only time one has ever loved. Difference of object does not alter singleness of passion. It merely intensifies it. We can have in life but one great experience at best, and the secret of life is to reproduce that experience as often as possible.'

'Even when one has been wounded by it, Harry?' asked the Duchess, after a pause.

'Especially when one has been wounded by it,' answered Lord Henry.

The Duchess turned and looked at Dorian Gray with a curious expression in her eyes. 'What do you say to that, Mr. Gray?' she inquired.

Dorian hesitated for a moment. Then he threw his head back and laughed. 'I always agree with Harry, Duchess.'

'Even when he is wrong?'

'Harry is never wrong, Duchess.'

'And does his philosophy make you happy?'

'I have never searched for happiness. Who wants happiness? I have searched for pleasure.'

'And found it, Mr. Gray?'

'Often. Too often.'

The Duchess sighed. 'I am searching for peace,' she said, 'and if I don't go and dress, I shall have none this evening.'

'Let me get you some orchids, Duchess,' cried Dorian, starting to his feet, and walking down the conservatory.

'You are flirting disgracefully with him,' said Lord Henry to his cousin. 'You had better take care. He is very fascinating.'

'If he were not, there would be no battle.'

'Greek meets Greek, then?'

'I am on the side of the Trojans. They fought for a woman.'

'They were defeated.'

'There are worse things than capture,' she answered.

'You gallop with a loose rein.'

'Pace gives life,' was the riposte.

'I shall write it in my diary tonight.'

'What?'

'That a burnt child loves the fire.'

'I am not even singed. My wings are untouched.'

'You use them for everything, except flight.'

'Courage has passed from men to women. It is a new experience for us.'

'You have a rival.'

'Who?'

He laughed. 'Lady Narborough,' he whispered. 'She perfectly adores him.'

'You fill me with apprehension. The appeal to Antiquity is fatal to us who are romanticists.'

'Romanticists! You have all the methods of science.'

'Men have educated us.'

'But not explained you.'

'Describe us as a sex,' was her challenge.

'Sphinxes without secrets.'

She looked at him, smiling. 'How long Mr. Gray is!' she said. 'Let us go and help him. I have not yet told him the colour of my frock.'

'Ah! you must suit your frock to his flowers, Gladys.'

'That would be a premature surrender.'

'Romantic Art begins with its climax.'

'I must keep an opportunity for retreat.'

'In the Parthian manner?'

'They found safety in the desert. I could not do that.'

From *The Picture of Dorian Gray*.

A SLIGHT MISUNDERSTANDING

By Canon Sheehan

FATHER LETHEBY commenced sooner than I expected.

I think it was about nine or ten days after his formal instalment in his new house, just as I was reading after breakfast the *Freeman's Journal* of two days past, the door of my parlour was suddenly flung open, a bunch of keys was thrown angrily on the table, and a voice (which I recognized as that of Mrs. Darcy, the chapel woman), strained to the highest tension of indignation, shouted:—

'There! and may there be no child to pray over my grave if ever I touch them again! Wisha! where in the world did you get him? or where did he come from, at all, at all? The son of a jook! the son of a draper over there at Kilkeel. Didn't Mrs. Morarty tell me how she sowld socks to his ould father? An' he comes here complaining of dacent people! "Dirt," sez he. "Where?" sez I. "There," sez he. "Where?" sez I. "I came of as dacent people as him. Wondher *you* never complained. But you're too aisy. You always allow these galivanters of curates to crow over you. But I tell you I won't stand it. If I had to beg my bread from house to house, I won't stand being told I'm dirty. Why, the ladies of the Great House said they could see their faces in the candlesticks; and didn't the Bishop say 'twas the natest vestry in the diocese? And this new cojutor with his gran' accent, which no one can understand, and his gran' furniture, and his whipster of a servant, begor, no one can stand him. We must all clear out. And, after me eighteen years, scrubbing, and washing, and ironing, wid me two little orphans, which that blackguard, Jem Darcy (the Lord have mercy on his sowl!) left me, must go to foreign countries to airn me bread, because I'm not good enough for his reverence.

59

Well, 'tis you'll be sorry. But, if you wint down on your two binded knees and said: "Mrs. Darcy, I deplore you to take them kays and go back to your juties," I wouldn't! No! Get some whipster that will suit his reverence. Mary Darcy isn't good enough.'

She left the room, only to return. She spoke with forced calmness.

'De thrifle of money you owe me, yer reverence, ye can sind it down to the house before I start for America. And dere's two glasses of althar wine in the bottle, and half a pound of candles.'

She went out again, but returned immediately.

'The surplus is over at Nell O'Brien's washing, and the black vestment is over at Tom Carmody's since the last station. The kay of the safe is under the door of the linny, to de left, and the chalice is in the basket, wrapped in the handkerchief. And, if you won't mind giving me a charackter, perhaps, Hannah will take it down in the evening.'

She went out again; but kept her hand on the door.

'Good-bye, your reverence, and God bless you! Sure, thin, you never said a hard word to a poor woman.' Then there was the sound of falling tears.

To all this tremendous philippic I never replied. I never do reply to a woman until I have my hand on the door handle and my finger on the key. I looked steadily at the column of stocks and shares on the paper, though I never read a word.

'This is rather a bad mess,' said I. 'He is coming out too strong.'

The minute particulars I had from Hannah soon after. Hannah and Mrs. Darcy are not friends. Two such village potentates could not be friends any more than two poets, or two critics, or two philosophers. As a rule, Hannah rather looked down on the chapel woman, and generally addressed her with studied politeness. 'How are you *today*, Mrs. Darcy?' or more frequently, 'Good *morning*, Mrs. Darcy.' On the other hand, Mary Darcy, as arbitress at stations, wakes, and weddings, had a wide influence in the parish, and I fear used to speak contemptuously sometimes of my housekeeper. But now there was what the newspapers call a Dual Alliance against the new-comers, and a stern determination that any attempt at superiority should be repressed with a firm hand, and to Mrs. Darcy's lot it fell to bear the martyrdom of high principle and to fire the first shot, that should be also the final one. And so it was, but not in the way Mrs. Darcy anticipated.

It would appear, then, that Father Letheby had visited the sacristy, and taken a most minute inventory of its treasures, and had, with all the zeal of a new reformer, found matters in a very bad state. Now, he was not one to smile benignantly at such irregularities and then throw the burden of correcting them on his pastor. He was outspoken and honest. He tore open drawers, and drew out their slimy, mildewed contents, sniffed ominously at the stuffy atmosphere, flung aside with gestures of contempt some of Mrs. Darcy's dearest treasures, such as a magnificent reredos of blue paper with gold stars; held up gingerly, and with curled lip, corporals and purificators, and wound up the awful inspection with the sentence:—

'I never saw such abominable filth in my life.'

Now, you may accuse us in Ireland of anything you please from coining to parricide, but if you don't want to see blazing eyes and hear vigorous language don't say Dirt. Mrs. Darcy bore the fierce scrutiny of her menage without shrinking, but when he mentioned the ugly word, all her fury shot forth, and it was all the more terrible, because veiled under a show of studied politeness.

'Dirt!' she said. 'I'd be plazed to see your reverence show one speck of dirt in the place.'

'Good heavens, woman!' he said, 'what do you mean? There is dirt everywhere, in the air, under my feet, in the grate, on the altar. It would take the Atlantic to purify the place.'

'You're the first gentleman that ever complained of the place,' said Mrs. Darcy. 'Of course, there aren't carpets, and bearskins, and cowhides, which are now the fashion, I believe. An' dere isn't a looking-glass, nor a pianney; but would your reverence again show me the dirt? A poor woman's charackter is all she has.'

'I didn't mean to impute anything to your character,' he said, mildly, 'but if you can't see that this place is frightfully dirty, I suppose I can't prove it. Look at that!'

He pointed to a gruesome heap of cinders, half-burnt papers, brown ashes, etc., that choked up the grate.

'Yerra. Glory be to God!' said Mrs. Darcy, appealing to an imaginary audience, 'he calls the sweepings of the altar, and the clane ashes, dirt. Yerra, what next?'

'This next,' he said, determinedly; 'come here.' He took her out and pointed to the altar cloth. It was wrinkled and grimy, God forgive me! and there were stars of all sizes and colours darkening it.

'Isn't that a disgrace to the Church?' he said, sternly.

'I see no disgrace in it,' said Mrs. Darcy. 'It was washed and made up last Christmas, and is as clane today as the day it came from the mangle.'

'Do you call that clean?' he shouted, pointing to the drippings of the candles.

'Yerra, what harm is that,' said she, 'a bit of blessed wax that fell from the candles? Sure, 'tis of that they make the Agnus Deis.'

'You're perfectly incorrigible,' he said. 'I'll report the whole wretched business to the parish priest, and let him deal with you.'

'Begor you may,' said she, 'but I'll have my story first.'

And so she had. Father Letheby gave me his version afterwards. He did so with the utmost delicacy, for it was all an indirect indictment of my own slovenliness and sinful carelessness. I listened with shamed face and bent head, and determined to let him have his way. I knew that Mrs. Darcy would not leave for America just yet.

But what was my surprise on the following Sunday, when, on entering the sacristy to prepare for Mass, I slid along a polished floor, and but for the wall would probably have left a vacancy at Kilronan to some expectant curate. The floor glinted and shone with wax; and there were dainty bits of fibre matting here and there. The grate was black-leaded, and there was a wonderful fire-screen with an Alpine landscape. The clock was clicking steadily, as if Time had not stood still for us all for many years: and there were my little altar boys in snowy surplices as neat as the acolytes that proffered soap and water to the Archbishop of Rheims, when he called for bell and book in the famous legend.

But oh! my anguish when I drew a stiff white amice over my head, instead of the dear old limp and wrinkled one I was used to; and when I feebly tried to push my hands through the lace meshes of an alb, that would stand with stiffness and pride, if I placed it on the floor, I would gladly have called for my old garment; but I knew that I too had to undergo the process of the new reformation; and, with much agony, I desisted. But I drew the line at a biretta which cut my temples with its angles, and I called out:—

'Mrs. Darcy.'

A young woman, with her hair all tidied up, and with a white apron, laced at the edges, and pinned to her breasts, came out from a recess. She was smiling bashfully, and appeared as if she would like to run away and hide somewhere.

'Mrs. Darcy,' I called again.

The young woman smiled more deeply, and said with a kind of smirk:—

'Here I am, your reverence!'

It is fortunate for me that I have acquired, after long practice, the virtue of silence; for when I recognized the voice of my old friend, I was thunderstruck. I'm sure I would have said something very emphatic, but my habits restrained me. But I regret to say it was all a source of distraction to me in the celebration of the Divine Mysteries, and during the day.

From *My New Curate*.

A DIGRESSION CONCERNING CRITICS

By Jonathan Swift

PAUSANIAS IS OF OPINION, that the perfection of writing correct was entirely owing to the institution of critics; and, that he can possibly mean no other than the true critic, is, I think, manifest enough from the following description. He says, they were a race of men, who delighted to nibble at the superfluities, and excrescences of books; which the learned at length observing, took warning, of their own accord, to lop the luxuriant, the rotten, the dead, the sapless, and the over-grown branches from their works. But now, all this he cunningly shades under the following allegory; that the Nauplians in Argia learned the art of pruning their vines, by observing that when an ASS has browsed upon one of them, it thrived the better, and bore fairer fruit. But Herodotus, holding the very same hieroglyph, speaks much plainer, and almost *in terminis*. He hath been so bold as to tax the true critics of ignorance and malice; telling us openly, for I think nothing can be plainer, that in the western part of Libya, there were ASSES with HORNS; upon which relation Ctesias yet refines, mentioning the very same animal about India, adding, that whereas all other ASSES wanted a gall, these horned ones were so redundant in that part, that their flesh was not to be eaten, because of its extreme bitterness.

Now, the reason why those ancient writers treated this subject only by types and figures, was, because they durst not make open attacks against a party so potent and terrible, as the critics of those ages were; whose very voice was so dreadful, that a legion of authors would tremble, and drop their pens at the sound; for so Herodotus tells us expressly in another place, how a vast army of Scythians was put to flight in a panic terror, by the braying of an ASS. From hence it is conjectured by

certain profound philologers, that the great awe and reverence
paid to a true critic, by the writers of Britain, have been derived
to us from those our Scythian ancestors. In short, this dread
was so universal, that in process of time, those authors, who had
a mind to publish their sentiments more freely, in describing
the true critics of their several ages, were forced to leave off
the use of the former hieroglyph, as too nearly approaching the
prototype, and invented other terms instead thereof, that
were more cautious and mystical. So, Diodorus, speaking
to the same purpose, ventures no farther, than to say, that in
the mountains of Helicon, there grows a certain weed, which
bears a flower of so damned a scent, as to poison those who
offer to smell it. Lucretius gives exactly the same relation:

Est etiam in magnis Heliconis montibus arbos,[1]
Floris adore hominem tetro consueta necare.

Lib. 6.

But Ctesias, whom we lately quoted, hath been a great deal
bolder; he had been used with much severity by the true critics
of his own age, and therefore could not forbear to leave behind
him, at least one deep mark of his vengeance against the whole
tribe. His meaning is so near the surface, that I wonder how
it possibly came to be overlooked by those who deny the antiquity
of true critics. For, pretending to make a description of many
strange animals about India, he hath set down these remarkable
words: 'Among the rest', says he, 'there is a serpent that wants
teeth, and consequently cannot bite; but if its vomit, (to which
it is much addicted), happens to fall upon anything, a certain
rottenness or corruption ensues. These serpents are generally
found among the mountains, where jewels grow, and they
frequently emit a poisonous juice: whereof whoever drinks,
that person's brains fly out of his nostrils.'
There was also among the ancients a sort of critics, not
distinguished in species from the former, but in growth or

---

[1] Near Helicon, and round the learned hill,
Grow trees, whose blossoms with their odour kill.

degree, who seem to have been only the tyros or junior scholars;
yet, because of their differing employments, they are frequently
mentioned as a sect by themselves. The usual exercise of
these younger students, was, to attend constantly at theatres,
and learn to spy out the worst parts of the play, whereof they
were obliged carefully to take note, and render a rational
account to their tutors. Fleshed at these smaller sports, like
young wolves, they grew up in time to be nimble and strong
enough for hunting down large game. For it hath been observed,
both among ancients and moderns, that a true critic hath one
quality in common with a whore and an alderman, never to
change his title or his nature; that a gray critic has been certainly
a green one, the perfections and acquirements of his age being
only the improved talents of his youth; like hemp, which some
naturalists inform us is bad for suffocations, though taken but
in the seed. I esteem the invention, or at least the refinement of
prologues, to have been owing to these younger proficients, of
whom Terence makes frequent and honourable mention, under
the name of *malevoli*.

Now, 'tis certain, the institution of the true critics was of
absolute necessity to the commonwealth of learning. For all
human actions seem to be divided, like Themistocles and his
company; one man can fiddle, and another can make a small
town a great city; and he that cannot do either one or the other,
deserves to be kicked out of the creation. The avoiding of
which penalty, has doubtless given the first birth to the nation
of critics; and withal, an occasion for their secret detractors to
report, that a true critic is a sort of mechanic, set up with a stock
and tools for his trade, at as little expense as a tailor; and that
there is much analogy between the utensils and abilities of both:
that the tailor's hell is the type of a critic's commonplace book,
and his wit and learning held forth by the goose; that it requires
at least as many of these to the making up of one scholar, as
of the others to the composition of a man; that the valour of
both is equal, and their weapons near of a size. Much may be
said in answer to those invidious reflections; and I can positively
affirm the first to be a falsehood: for, on the contrary, nothing

is more certain, than that it requires greater layings out, to be free of the critic's company, than of any other you can name. For, as to be a true beggar, it will cost the richest candidate every groat he is worth; so, before one can commence a true critic, it will cost a man all the good qualities of his mind; which, perhaps for a less purchase, would be thought but an indifferent bargain.

Having thus amply proved the antiquity of criticism, and described the primitive state of it, I shall now examine the present condition of this empire, and shew how well it agrees with its ancient self. A certain author, whose works have many ages since been entirely lost, does, in his fifth book, and eighth chapter, say of critics, that their writings are the mirrors of learning. This I understand in a literal sense, and suppose our author must mean, that whoever designs to be a perfect writer, must inspect into the books of critics, and correct his invention there, as in a mirror. Now, whoever considers, that the mirrors of the ancients were made of brass, and *sine mercurio*, may presently apply the two principal qualifications of a true modern critic, and consequently must needs conclude, that these have always been, and must be for ever the same. For brass is an emblem of duration, and, when it is skilfully burnished, will cast reflections from its own superficies, without any assistance of mercury from behind. All the other talents of a critic will not require a particular mention, being included, or easily deducible to these. However, I shall conclude with three maxims, which serve both as characteristics to distinguish a true modern critic from a pretender, and will be also of admirable use to those worthy spirits, who engage in so useful and honourable an art.

The first is, that criticism, contrary to all other faculties of the intellect, is ever held the truest and best, when it is the very first result of the critic's mind; as fowlers reckon the first aim for the surest, and seldom fail of missing the mark, if they stay for a second.

Secondly, the true critics are known, by their talents of swarming about the noblest writers, to which they are carried merely by instinct, as a rat to the best cheese, or a wasp to the fairest fruit. So when the king is on horse-back, he is sure to be the dirtiest person of the company; and they that make their court best, are such as bespatter him most.

Lastly, a true critic, in the perusal of a book, is like a dog at a feast, whose thoughts and stomach are wholly set upon what the guests fling away, and consequently is apt to snarl most when there are the fewest bones.

Thus much, I think, is sufficient to serve by way of address to my patrons, the true modern critics; and may very well atone for my past silence, as well as that which I am like to observe for the future. I hope I have deserved so well of their whole body, as to meet with generous and tender usage from their hands.

From *A Tale of a Tub*.

THE MEET OF THE BEAGLES

By H. de Vere Stackpoole

DIRECTLY Patsy had left the news that the 'quality' were coming to the meet and returned to the house the crowd in front of the Castle Knock Inn thickened.

Word of the impending event went from cabin to cabin, and Mr. Mahony, the chimney sweep, put his head out of his door.

'What's the news, Rafferty?' cried Mr. Mahony.

'Mimber of Parlymint and all the quality comin' to the meet!' cried a ragged-looking ruffian who was running by.

'Sure, it'll be a big day for Shan Finucane,' said Mrs. Mahony, who was standing behind her husband in the doorway with a baby in her arms.

Mr. Mahony said nothing for a while, but watched the crowd in front of the inn.

'Look at him,' said Mr. Mahony, breaking out at last—'look at him in his ould green coat! Look at him with the ould whip undher his arm, and the boots on his feet not paid for, and him struttin' about as if he was the Marqus of Waterford! Holy Mary! did yiz ever see such an objick? Mr. Mullins!'

'Halloo!' replied Mr. Mullins, the cobbler across the way, who, with his window open owing to the mildness of the weather, was whaling away at a shoe-sole, the only busy man in the village.

'Did y' hear the news?'

'What news?'

'Shan's going to get a new coat.'

'Faith, thin, I hope he'll pay first for his ould shoes.'

'How much does he owe you?'

'Siven and six—bad cess to him!'

'He'll pay you tonight, if he doesn't drink the money first, for there's a Mimber of Parlymint goin' to the meet, and he'll most like put a suverin in the poor box.'

69

Mr. Mullins made no reply, but went on whaling away at his shoe, and Bob Mahony, having stepped into his cottage for a light for his pipe, came back and took up his post again at the door.

The crowd round the inn was growing bigger and bigger. Sneer as he might, Mr. Mahony could not but perceive that Shan was having the centre of the stage, a worshipping audience, and free drinks.

Suddenly he turned to his offspring, who were crowding behind him, and singling out Billy, the eldest:

'Put the dunkey to,' said Mr. Mahony.

'Sure, daddy,' cried the boy in astonishment, 'it's only the tarriers.'

'Put the dunkey to!' thundered his father, 'or it's the end of me belt I'll be brightenin' your intellects with.'

'There's two big bags of sut in the cart and the brushes,' said Billy, as he made off to do as he was bidden.

'Lave them in,' said Mr. Mahony; it's only the tarriers.'

In a few minutes the donkey, whose harness was primitive and composed mainly of rope, was put to, and the vehicle was at the door.

'Bob!' cried his wife as he took his seat.

'What is it?' asked Mr. Mahony, taking the reins.

'Won't you be afther givin' your face the lick of a tow'l?'

'It's only the tarriers,' replied Mr. Mahony; sure, I'm clane enough for them. Come up wid you, Norah.'

Norah, the small donkey, whose ears had been cocking this way and that, picked up her feet, and the vehicle, which was not much bigger than a costermonger's barrow, started.

At this moment, also, Shan and the dogs and the crowd were getting into motion, making down the road for Glen Druid gates.

'Hulloo! hulloo! hulloo!' cried Mr. Mahony, as he rattled up behind in the cart, 'where are yiz off to?'

'The meet of the baygles,' replied twenty voices; whilst Shan, who had heard his enemy's voice, stalked on, surrounded by his dogs, his old, battered hunting horn in one hand, and his whip under his arm.

'And where are they going to meet?' asked Mr. Mahony.

'Glen Druid gate,' replied the camp followers. There's a Mimber of Parlymint comin', and all the quality from the Big House.'

'Faith,' said Mr. Mahony, 'I thought there was somethin' up, for, by the look of Shan, as he passed me house this mornin', I thought he'd swallowed the Lord Liftinant, Crown ·jew'ls and all. Helloo! helloo! hulloo! make way for me carridge! Who are you crowdin'? Don't you know the Earl of Leinsther when y' see him? Out of the way, or I'll call me futman to disparse yiz.'

Shan heard it all, but marched on. He could have killed Bob Mahony, who was turning his triumph into a farce, but he contented himself with letting fly with his whip amongst the dogs, and blowing a note on his horn.

'What's that nize?' enquired Mr. Mahony, with a wink at the delighted crowd tramping beside the donkey cart.

'Shan's blowin' his harn,' yelled the rabble.

'Faith, I thought it was Widdy Finnegan's rooster he was carryin' in the tail pockit of his coat,' said the humorist.

The crowd roared at this conceit, which was much more pungent and pointed as delivered in words by Mr. Mahony; but Shan, to all appearances, was deaf.

The road opposite the park gates was broad and shadowed by huge elm trees, which gave the spot in summer the darkness and coolness of a cave. Here Shan halted, the crowd halted, and the donkey-cart drew up.

Mr. Mahony tapped the dottle out of his pipe carefully on the rail of his cart, filled the pipe, replaced the dottle on the top of the tobacco, and drew a whiff.

The clock of Glen Druid House struck ten, and the notes came floating over park and trees; not that anyone heard them, for the yelping of the dogs and the noise of the crowd filled the quiet country road with the hubbub of a fair.

'What's that you were axing me?' cried Mr. Mahony to a supposed interrogator in the crowd. 'Is the Prince o' Wales comin'? No, he ain't. I had a tellygrum from him this mornin' sendin' his excuzes. Will some gintleman poke that rat-terrier

out that's got under the wheels of me carridge—out, you baste!'
He leaned over and hit a rabbit-beagle that had strayed under
the donkey-cart a tip with his stick. The dog, though not hurt,
for Bob Mahony was much too good a sportsman to hurt an
animal, gave a yelp.

Shan turned at the sound, and his rage exploded.

'Who are yiz hittin'?' cried Shan.

'I'm larnin' your dogs manners,' replied Bob.

The huntsman surveyed the sweep, the cart, the soot bags,
and the donkey.

'I beg your pardin',' said he, touchin' his hat, 'I didn't see
you at first for the sut.'

Mr. Mahony took his short pipe from his mouth, put it back
upside down, shoved his old hat further back on his head,
rested his elbows on his knees, and contemplated Shan.

'But it's glad I am,' went on Shan, 'you've come to the meet
and brought a mimber of the family with you.'

Fate was against Bob Mahony, for at that moment Norah
scenting another of her species in a field near by, curled her lip
stiffened her legs, projected her head, rolled her eyes, and
'let a bray out of her' that almost drowned the howls of laughter
from the exulting mob.

But Shan Finucane did not stir a muscle of his face, and
Bob Mahony's fixed sneer did not flicker or waver.

'Don't mention it, mum,' said Shan, taking off his old cap
when the last awful, rasping, despairing note of the bray had
died down into silence.

Another howl from the onlookers, which left Mr. Mahony
unmoved.

'They get on well together,' said he, addressing an imaginary
acquaintance in the crowd.

'Whist and hould your nize, and let's hear what else they
have to say to wan another.'

Suddenly, and before Shan Finucane could open his lips,
a boy who had been looking over the rails into the park, yelled:

'Here's the Mimber of Parlymint—here they come—Hurroo!'

'Now, then,' said the huntsman, dropping repartee and

seizing the sweep's donkey by the bridle, 'sweep yourselves off, and don't be disgracin' the hunt wid your sut bags and your dirty faces—away wid yiz!'

'The hunt!' yelled Mahony, with a burst of terrible laughter. 'Listen to him and his ould rat-terriers callin' thim a hunt! Lave go of the dunkey!'

'Away wid yiz!'

'Lave go of the dunkey, or I'll batter the head of you in wid me stick! Lave go of the dunkey!'

Suddenly seizing the long flue brush beside him, and disengaging it from the bundle of sticks with which it was bound, he let fly with the bristle end of it at Shan, and Shan, catching his heel on a stone, went over flat on his back in the road.

In a second he was up, whip in hand; in a second Mr. Mahony was down, a bag half-filled with soot—a terrible weapon of assault—in his fist.

'Harns! harns!' yelled Mahony, mad with the spirit of battle, and unconsciously chanting the fighting cry of long-forgotten ancestors. 'Who says cruckeder than a ram's harn!'

'Go it, Shan!' yelled the onlookers. 'Give it him, Bob—sut him in the face—Butt-end the whip, y'idgit—Hurroo! Hurroo! Holy Mary! he nearly landed him then—Mind the dogs—'

Armed with the soot-bag swung like a club, and the old hunting-whip butt-ended, the two combatants formed the centre of a circle of yelling admirers.

'Look!' said Miss Lestrange, as the party from the house came in view of the road. 'Look at the crowd and the two men!'

'They're fighting!' cried the general. 'I believe the ruffians dared to have the impudence to start fighting!'

At this moment came the noise of wheels from behind, and the 'tub', which had obtained permission to go to the meet, drew up, with Patsy driving the children.

'Let the children remain here,' said the General. 'You stay with them, Violet. Come along, Boxall, till we see what these ruffians mean.'

So filled was his mind with the objects in view that he quite forgot Dicky Fanshawe.

'You have put on the short skirt,' said Dicky, who at that moment would scarcely have turned his head twice or given a second thought had the battle of Austerlitz been in full blast beyond the park palings.

'And my thick boots,' said Violet, pushing forward a delightful little boot to speak for itself.

The children were so engaged watching the proceedings on the road that they had no eyes or ears for their elders.

'Have you ever been beagling before?' asked Dicky.

'Never; but I've been paper-chasing.'

'You can get through a hedge?'

'Rather!'

'That'll do,' said Dicky.

'Mr. Fanshawe,' cried Lord Gawdor from the 'tub', 'look at the chaps in the road—aren't they going for each other!'

'I see,' said Mr. Fanshawe, whose back was to the road—'Violet——'

'Yes.'

'No one's looking—'

'That doesn't matter—No—not here—Dicky, if you don't behave, I'll get into the tub—Gracious! what's that?'

'He's down!' cried Patsy, who had been standing up to see better.

'Who?' asked Mr. Fanshawe.

'The Mimber of Parlymint—Misther Boxall—Bob Mahony's grassed him—'

'They're all fighting!' cried Violet. 'Come, Mr. Fanshawe—Patsy—' She started for the gates at a run.

When the General had arrived on the scene, Shan had just got in and landed his antagonist a drum-sounding blow on the ribs with the butt of his whip.

'Seize the other chap, Boxall!' cried General Grampound, making for Mahony.

He was just half a second too late; the soot bag, swung like a club, missed Shan, and, catching Mr. Boxall fair and square on the side of the face, sent him spinning like a tee-totum across the road, and head over heels into the ditch.

That was all.

A dead silence took the yelling crowd.

'He's kilt!' came a voice.

'He isn't; sure, his legs is wavin'.'

'Who is he?'

'He's the Mimber of Parlymint! Run for your life, and don't lave off runnin' till you're out of the country.'

'Hold your tongue!' cried General Grampound. 'Boxall—hullo! Boxall! are you hurt?'

'I'm all right,' replied Mr. Boxall, who, from being legs upwards, was now on hands and knees in the ditch. 'I've lost something—dash it!'

'What have you lost?'

'Watch.'

'Come out and I'll get some of these chaps to look.'

Mr. Boxall came out of the ditch with his handkerchief held to the left side of his forehead.

'Why, your watch and chain are on you!' cried the General.

'So they are,' said Mr. Boxall, pulling the watch out with his left hand, and putting it back. 'I'm off to the house—I want to wash.'

'Sure you're not hurt?'

'Not in the least, only my forehead scratched.'

'What's up?' cried Dicky Fanshawe, who had just arrived.

'Nothing,' replied his uncle. 'Fellow hit him by mistake—no bones broken. Will you take the governess cart back to the house, Boxall?'

'No, thanks—I'll walk.'

'His legs is all right,' murmured the sympathetic crowd, as the injured one departed still with his handkerchief to his face, 'and his arums. Sure, it's the mercy and all his neck wasn't bruck.'

'Did yiz see the skelp Bob landed him?'

'Musha! Sure, I thought it would have sent his head flying into Athy, like a gulf ball.'

Patsy, who had pulled the governess cart up, rose to his feet; his sharp eye had caught sight of something lying on the road.

'Hould the reins a moment, Mr. Robert,' said he, putting them into Lord Gawdor's hands. He hopped out of the cart, picked up the object in the road, whatever it was, put it in his trousers' pocket, and then stood holding the pony's head; whilst the Meet, from which Bob Mahony had departed as swiftly as his donkey could trot, turned its attention to the business of the day, and Shan, collecting his dogs, declared his intention of drawing the Furzes.

'Was that a marble you picked up, Patsy?' asked Lord Gawdor, as the red-headed one, hearing Shan's declaration, climbed into the 'tub' again and took the reins.

Patsy grinned.

*   *   *   *   *   *   *

Meanwhile Mr. Fanshawe had been writing three important letters in the library. When he had finished and carefully sealed them, he placed them one on top of the other, and looked at his watch.

The three letters he had just written would make everything all right at the other end. This was the hot end of the poker, and it had to be grasped.

Patsy was the person who would help him to grasp it. Patsy he felt to be a tower of strength and 'cuteness,' if such a simile is permissible. And, rising from the writing-table and putting the letters in his pocket, he went to find Patsy. He had not far to go, for as he came into the big hall Patsy was crossing it with a tray in hand.

'Patsy,' said Mr. Fanshawe, 'when does the post go out?'

'If you stick your letters in the letter box be the hall door, sir,' said Patsy, 'it will be cleared in half-an-hour. Jim Murphy takes the letter-bag to Castle Knock.'

'Right!' said Mr. Fanshawe. 'And, see here, Patsy!'

'Yes, sir?'

'I'm in a bit of a fix, Patsy, and you may be able to help.'

'And what's the fix, sir?' asked Patsy.

'You know the young lady you gave the note to this morning —by the way, how did you give it?'

'I tried to shove it undher her door, sir.'

'Yes?'

'It wouldn't go, so I gave a knock. "Who's there?" says she.

"No one," says I; "it's only hot water I'm bringin' you," for, you see, sir, the ould missis, her ladyship, was in the next room, and she's not as deaf as she looks, and it's afraid I was, every minnit, her door'd open, and she and her ear-trumpet come out in the passidge. "I have hot wather," says she. "Niver mind," says I, "this is betther. Open the door, for the love of God, for I can't get it under the door, unless I rowl it up and shove it through the keyhole." Wid that she opens the door a crack and shoves her head out. "Who's it from?" she says. "I don't know," says I; "it's just a letther I found on the stairs I thought might belong to you." "Thanks," says she, "it does," and wid that she shut the door, and I left her.'

'Well, see here, Patsy!'

'Yes, sir?'

'I'm going to marry Miss Lestrange.'

'Faith, and I guessed that,' said Patsy; 'and it's I that'd be joyful to dance at your weddin', sir.'

'There won't be any dancing in the business,' said Mr. Fanshawe, grimly. 'You know Mr. Boxall, Patsy?'

'The Mimber of Parlymint?'

'Yes. Well, he wants to marry Miss Lestrange; and the worst of it is, Patsy, that my uncle, General Grampound, wants him to marry her, too.'

'Yes, sir,' said Patsy. 'And, Mr. Fanshawe.'

'Yes?'

'I forget to tell you, sir, you needn't be afear'd of Mr. Boxall for the next few days.'

'How's that?'

'When Bob Mahony hit him the skelp on the head wid the sut bag, his eye popped out of his head on the road.'

'His what?—Oh, I remember—'

'Finders is keepers, sir,' said Patsy, with a grin.

'Why, good heavens—you don't mean to say—'

'I've got his eye in my pocket, sir,' said Patsy, in a hoarse whisper. 'He's sint a telygram for another wan but till it comes he's tethered to his bed like a horse to a—'

'That's enough—that's enough,' said Mr. Fanshaw. 'Here's half a crown for you, Patsy, for—carrying my cartridges.'

From *Patsy*.

LISHEEN RACES, SECOND HAND

By E. Œ. Somerville and Martin Ross

HAD IT NOT BEEN for a large stone lying on the road, and had the filly not chosen to swerve so as to bring the wheel on top of it, I dare say we might have got to the races; but by an unfortunate coincidence both these things occurred, and when we recovered from the consequent shock, the tire of one of the wheels had come off, and was trundling with cumbrous gaiety into the ditch. Flurry stopped the filly and began to laugh; Leigh Kelway said something startlingly unparliamentary under his breath.

'Well, it might be worse,' Flurry said consolingly as he lifted the tire on to the car; 'we're not half a mile from a forge.'

We walked that half-mile in funereal procession behind the car; the glory had departed from the weather, and an ugly wall of cloud was rising up out of the west to meet the sun; the hills had darkened and lost colour, and the white bog cotton shivered in a cold wind that smelt of rain.

By a miracle the smith was not at the races, owing, as he explained, to his having 'the toothaches', the two facts combined producing in him a morosity only equalled by that of Leigh Kelway. The smith's sole comment on the situation was to unharness the filly, and drag her into the forge, where he tied her up. He then proceeded to whistle viciously on his fingers in the direction of a cottage, and to command, in tones of thunder, some unseen creature to bring over a couple of baskets of turf. The turf arrived in process of time, on a woman's back, and was arranged in a circle in a yard at the back of the forge. The tire was bedded in it, and the turf was with difficulty kindled at different points.

'Ye'll not get to the races this day,' said the smith, yielding to a sardonic satisfaction; 'the turf's wet, and I haven't one to

78

do a hand's turn for me.' He laid the wheel on the ground and lit his pipe.

Leigh Kelway looked pallidly about him over the spacious empty landscape of brown mountain slopes patched with golden furze and seamed with grey walls; I wondered if he were as hungry as I. We sat on stones opposite the smouldering ring of turf and smoked, and Flurry beguiled the smith into grim and calumnious confidences about every horse in the country. After about an hour, during which the turf went out three times, and the weather became more and more threatening, a girl with a red petticoat over her head appeared at the gate of the yard, and said to the smith:

'The horse is gone away from ye.'

'Where?' exclaimed Flurry, springing to his feet.

'I met him walking wesht the road there below, and when I thought to turn him he commenced to gallop.'

'Pulled her head out of the headstall,' said Flurry, after a rapid survey of the forge. 'She's near home by now.'

It was at this moment that the rain began; the situation could scarcely have been better stage-managed. After reviewing the position, Flurry and I decided that the only thing to do was to walk to a public-house a couple of miles farther on, feed there if possible, hire a car, and go home.

It was an uphill walk, with mild generous raindrops striking thicker and thicker on our faces; no one talked, and the grey clouds crowded up from behind the hills like billows of steam. Leigh Kelway bore it all with egregious resignation. I cannot pretend that I was at heart sympathetic, but by virtue of being his host I felt responsible for the breakdown, for his light suit, for everything, and divined his sentiment of horror at the first sight of the public-house.

It was a long, low cottage, with a line of dripping elm trees overshadowing it; empty cars and carts round its door, and a babel from within made it evident that the race-goers were pursuing a gradual homeward route. The shop was crammed with steaming countrymen, whose loud brawling voices, all talking together, roused my English friend to his first remark since we had left the forge.

'Surely, Yeates, we are not going into that place?' he said severely: 'those men are all drunk.'

'Ah, nothing to signify!' said Flurry, plunging in and driving his way through the throng like a plough. 'Here, Mary Kate!' he called to the girl behind the counter, 'tell your mother we want some tea and bread and butter in the room inside.'

The smell of bad tobacco and spilt porter was choking; we worked our way through it after him towards the end of the shop, intersecting at every hand discussions about the races.

'Tom was very nice. He spared his horse all along, and then he put into him—' 'Well, at Goggin's corner the third horse was before the second, but he was goin' wake in himself.' 'I tell ye the mare had the hind leg fasht in the fore.' 'Clancy was dipping in the saddle.' ' 'Twas a dam nice race whatever——'

We gained the inner room at last, a cheerless apartment, adorned with sacred pictures, a sewing-machine, and an array of supplementary tumblers and wineglasses; but, at all events, we had it so far to ourselves. At intervals during the next half-hour Mary Kate burst in with cups and plates, cast them on the table and disappeared, but of food there was no sign. After a further period of starvation and of listening to the noise in the shop, Flurry made a sortie, and, after lengthy and unknown adventures, reappeared carrying a huge brown teapot, and driving before him Mary Kate with the remainder of the repast. The bread tasted of mice, the butter of turf-smoke, the tea of brown paper, but we had got past the critical stage. I had entered upon my third round of bread and butter when the door was flung open, and my valued acquaintance, Slipper, slightly advanced in liquor, presented himself to our gaze. His bandy legs sprawled consequentially, his nose was redder than a coal of fire, his prominent eyes rolled crookedly upon us, and his left hand swept behind him the attempt of Mary Kate to frustrate his entrance.

'Good-evening to my vinerable friend, Mr. Flurry Knox!' he began, in the voice of a town crier, 'and to the Honourable Major Yeates, and the English gintleman!'

This impressive opening immediately attracted an audience

from the shop, and the doorway filled with grinning faces as Slipper advanced farther into the room.

'Why weren't ye at the races, Mr. Flurry?' he went on, his roving eye taking a grip of us all at the same time; 'sure the Miss Bennetts and all the ladies was asking where were ye.'

'It'd take some time to tell them that,' said Flurry, with his mouth full; 'but what about the races, Slipper? Had you good sport?'

'Sport is it? Divil so pleasant an afternoon ever you seen,' replied Slipper. He leaned against a side table, and all the glasses on it jingled. 'Does your honour know O'Driscoll?' he went on irrelevantly. 'Sure you do. He was in your honour's stable. It's what we were all sayin'; it was a great pity your honour was not there, for the likin' you had to Driscoll.'

'That's thrue,' said a voice at the door.

'There wasn't one in the Barony but was gethered in it, through and fro,' continued Slipper, with a quelling glance at the interrupter; 'and there was tints for sellin' porther, and whisky as pliable as new milk, and boys goin' round the tints outside, feeling for heads with the big ends of their blackthorns, and all kinds of recreations, and the Sons of Liberty's piffler and dhrum band from Skebawn; though faith! there was more of thim runnin' to look at the races than what was playin' in it; not to mintion different occasions that the bandmasther was atin' his lunch within in the whisky tint.'

'But what about Driscoll?' said Flurry.

'Sure it's about him I'm tellin' ye,' replied Slipper, with the practised orator's watchful eye on his growing audience. ' 'Twas within in the same whisky tint meself was, with the bandmasther and a few of the lads, an' we buyin' a ha'porth o' crackers, when I seen me brave Driscoll landin' into the tint, and a pair o' thim long boots on him; him that hadn't a shoe nor a stocking to his foot when your honour had him picking grass out o' the stones behind in your yard. "Well," says I to meself, "we'll knock some spoort out of Driscoll!"

' "Come here to me, acushla!" says I to him; "I suppose it's some way wake in the legs y'are," says I, "an' the docthor put them on ye the way the people wouldn't thrample ye!"

' "May the divil choke ye!" says he, pleasant enough, but I knew by the blush he had he was vexed.

' "Then I suppose 'tis a left-tenant colonel y'are," says I; "yer mother must be proud out o' ye!" says I, "an' maybe ye'll lend her a loan o' thim waders when she's rinsin' yer bauneen in the river!" says I.

' "There'll be work out o' this!" says he, lookin' at me both sour and bitther.

' "Well indeed, I was thinkin' you were blue moulded for want of a batin'," says I. He was for fightin' us then, but afther we had him pacificated with about a quarther of a naggin o' sperrits, he told us he was goin' ridin' in a race.

' "An' what'll ye ride?" says I.

' "Owld Bocock's mare," says he.

' "Knipes!" says I, sayin' a great curse; "is it that little staggeen from the mountains; sure she's somethin' about the one age with meself," says I. "Many's the time Jamesy Geoghegan and meself used to be dhrivin' her to Macroom with pigs an' all soorts,' says I; "an' is it leppin' stone walls ye want her to go now?"

' "Faith, there's walls and every vari'ty of obstackle in it," says he.

' "It'll be the best o' your play, so," says I, "to leg it away home out o' this."

' "An' who'll ride her, so?" says he.

' "Let the divil ride her," says I.'

Leigh Kelway, who had been leaning back seemingly half asleep, obeyed the hypnotism of Slipper's gaze, and opened his eyes.

'That was now all the conversation that passed between himself and meself,' resumed Slipper, 'and there was no great delay afther that till they said there was a race startin' and the dickens a one at all was goin' to ride only two, Driscoll, and one Clancy. With that then I seen Mr. Kinahane, the Petty Sessions clerk, goin' round clearin' the coorse, an' I gathered a few o' the neighbours, an' we walked the fields hither and over till we seen the most of th' obstackles.

' "Stand aisy now by the plantation," says I; "if they get to come as far as this, believe me ye'll see spoort," says I, "an' 'twill be a convenient spot to encourage the mare if she's anyway wake in herself," says I, cuttin' somethin' about five foot of an ash sapling out o' the plantation.

' "That's yer sort!" says owld Bocock, that was thravellin' the racecoorse, peggin' a bit o' paper down with a thorn in front of every lep, the way Driscoll 'd know the handiest place to face her at it.

'Well, I hadn't barely thrimmed the ash plant——'

'Have you any jam, Mary Kate?' interrupted Flurry, whose meal had been in no way interfered with by either the story or the highly-scented crowd who had come to listen to it.

'We have no jam, only thraycle, sir,' replied the invisible Mary Kate.

'I hadn't the switch barely thrimmed,' repeated Slipper firmly, 'when I heard the people screechin', an' I seen Driscoll an' Clancy comin' on, leppin' all before them, an' owld Bocock's mare bellusin' an' powdherin' along, an' bedad! whatever obstackle wouldn't throw *her* down, faith, she'd throw *it* down, an' there's the thraffic they had in it.

' "I declare to me sowl," says I, "if they continue on this way there's a great chance some one o' thim 'll win," says I.

' "Ye lie!" says the bandmasther, bein' a thrifle fulsome after his luncheon.

' "I do not," says I, "in regard of seein' how soople them two boys is. Ye might observe," says I, "that if they have no convenient way to sit on the saddle, they'll ride the neck o' the horse till such time as they gets an occasion to lave it," says I.

' "Arrah, shut your mouth!" says the bandmasther; "they're puckin' out this way now, an' may the divil admire me!" says he, "but Clancy has the other bet out, and the divil such leatherin' and beltin' of owld Bocock's mare ever you seen as what's in it!" says he.

'Well, when I seen them comin' to me, and Driscoll about the length of the plantation behind Clancy, I leta couple of bawls.

' "Skelp her, ye big brute!" says I. "What good's in ye that ye aren't able to skelp her"?'

The yell and the histrionic flourish of his stick with which Slipper delivered this incident brought down the house. Leigh Kelway was sufficiently moved to ask me in an undertone if 'skelp' was a local term.

'Well, Mr. Flurry, and gintlemen,' recommenced Slipper, 'I declare to ye when owld Bocock's mare heard thim roars she sthretched out her neck like a gandher, and when she passed me out she give a couple of grunts, and looked at me as ugly as a Christian.

' "Hah!" says I, givin' her a couple o' dhraws o' th' ash plant across the butt o' the tail, the way I wouldn't blind her; "I'll make ye grunt!" says I, "I'll nourish ye!"

'I knew well she was very frightful of th' ash plant since the winter Tommeen Sullivan had her under a sidecar. But now, in place of havin' any obligations to me, ye'd be surprised if ye heard the blaspheemious expressions of that young boy that was ridin' her; and whether it was over-anxious he was, turnin' around the way I'd hear him cursin', or whether it was some slither or slide came to owld Bocock's mare, I dunno, but she was bet up agin the last obstackle but two, and before ye could say "Schnipes," she was standin' on her two ears beyond in th' other field! I declare to ye, on the vartue of me oath, she stood that way till she reconnoithered what side would Driscoll fall, an' she turned about then and rolled on him as cosy as if he was meadow grass!'

Slipper stopped short; the people in the doorway groaned appreciatively; Mary Kate murmured 'The Lord save us!'

'The blood was dhruv out through his nose and ears,' continued Slipper, with a voice that indicated the cream of the narration, 'and you'd hear his bones crackin' on the ground! You'd have pitied the poor boy.'

'Good heavens!' said Leigh Kelway, sitting up very straight in his chair.

'Was he hurt, Slipper?' asked Flurry casually.

'Hurt is it?' echoed Slipper in high scorn; 'killed on the spot!' He paused to relish the effect of the *denouement* on Leigh Kelway. 'Oh, divil so pleasant an afthernoon ever you seen; and indeed,

Mr. Flurry, it's what we were all sayin', it was a great pity your honour was not there for the likin' you had for Driscoll.'

As he spoke the last word there was an outburst of singing and cheering from a car-load of people who had just pulled up at the door. Flurry listened, leaned back in his chair, and began to laugh.

'It scarcely strikes one as a comic incident,' said Leigh Kelway, very coldly to me; 'in fact, it seems to me that the police ought—'

'Show me Slipper!' bawled a voice in the shop; 'show me that dirty little undher-looper till I have his blood! Hadn't I the race won only for he souring the mare on me! What's that you say? I tell ye he did! He left seven slaps on her with the handle of a hay-rake——'

There was in the room in which we were sitting a second door, leading to the back yard, a door consecrated to the unobtrusive visits of so-called 'Sunday travellers'. Through it Slipper faded away like a dream, and, simultaneously, a tall young man, with a face like a red-hot potato tied up in a bandage, squeezed his way from the shop into the room.

'Well, Driscoll,' said Flurry, 'since it wasn't the teeth of the rake he left on the mare, you needn't be talking!'

Leigh Kelway looked from one to the other with a wilder expression in his eye than I had thought it capable of. I read in it a resolve to abandon Ireland to her fate.

From *Experiences of an Irish R.M.*

OUT OF ALL BOOKS

By Edward J. Delaney

WE CLOSED THE SCHOOL YEAR with the usual summer tests, which fill Teacher's Return No. 2 with ingenuous V.G.'s, and save us writing a week's syllabus. Johnny, who never lets us down, was faithfully present. From his infancy his mother abhorred separation from Johnny, who was an incurable martyr to 'a wind in the stomach', usually ascribed to the reactionary properties of 'th' oul' spuds'; but ever to the rescue in our hours of academic extremity she dutifully sent him in for every examination. Now he is fourteen and 'out of all books,' so this was in the nature of a valedictory appearance.

This year he was a candidate for Confirmation, and though in consequence he had some reasonably regular weeks of attendance to his credit, he was my principal heartache, with an elasticity of views on matters of doctrine not yet accorded general approval. His forte was homely narration of Bible stories. When I interrupted his highly colloquial account of the Last Supper to ask: 'Why did St. Peter say "Thou shalt never wash my feet"?' he hopefully replied: 'Because his feet were clane.' And on the great day, when with good fortune foreign to his kind, he emerged triumphantly from the Archiepiscopal encounter having been given no deeper problem to solve than 'Who made the world?' he looked at me reproachfully as he returned to his seat, animated, no doubt, with contemptuous thoughts of my frenzied endeavours to pierce his defences with the Impediments to Marriage, the different oaths, the various sacrileges, and other abstruse and extraneous matters entirely beyond his simple requirements.

Now with three months of attendance to his credit an examination in composition was a stimulating challenge. Forgotten

86

were his former incondite wrestlings with the difficulties of authorship, forgotten our frequent disputations on the absence of harmony between his nouns and verbs. He hitched up his precariously-held pants, dipped his pen to the muddiest depths, shook the surplus all over the desk, and marshalled his talents to the all-engrossing task of copying from his neighbour. But when I prescribed a separate subject for each he gave me an eye which said plainer than words that I could never be any thing in his life but a constant source of disappointment. I required him to state solo his views on the hackneyed subject of Holidays. Though it was a topic on which the roll book revealed him an authority he decided to rely almost completely on my prefatory remarks. He lugubriously wrote 'Holadays' at the top of the page, scowled at it sideways and likewise at me, and after a series of scowls exactly similar to the earlier ones, laboriously delivered himself of this masterpiece, which demonstrated that the seed I had previously scattered fell entirely on arable ground.

Holadays was invinted by the Irish Tworist Assosation who lives in Killarney and other seaside places and they are good for us because we do not live their all the year round and we have no change and cannot be healthy if we do not go away and some howtels are now also very clean. Butter is scarce and they are good for everybodey including howtels to make the Irish people stay at home because there is a awful war going on and we are newteral and we are praying for peace because we are not in it. Everyone must bring our rashen books to get coopens for our tea which is also scarce because it cannot be got. Only in the black market and that is a sin if you can help it. I like holadays but we have not much butter which is better than boms my mother do not like holadays because she said we will not have a stich of cloths left on us for school. I likes holadays because I can go for cigorets for my father.'

Meanwhile his neighbour Paddy was deep in a much more ambitious effort. He it was who, earlier in the morning, being examined as to sundry items of the previous week concerning Goldsmith, made a herculean attempt to recall the title of that worthy's famous play, when after intense research in the archives of his memory, he blurted out: 'The Drooping Woman.' Macaulay, we are told, could as a boy repeat verbatim poems he had read but once. Paddy could go one better, for he could produce impromptu a series of new and untrammelled versions, no matter how often he cramped his style by conning the original. Now in exercise of his unique gift he was committing to paper a tender prose rendering of Kickham's 'Irish Peasant Girl', and after forty-five minutes, with a perspiring nose and a protruding tongue, both necessary accompaniments to literary achievement on his part, he gave English letters the following:

We have a song in school about a Irish peasant girl who went to America for to get money. All the people in Ireland had to go to a foreign land. They had to pay a high rent. If the Irish people did not go to foreign countries a lot of the Irish would die with the hunger. One of them was the Irish peasant girl. This girl lived beside the Anner. Her father was dead and her mother was a widow and she had a lot of children. It was lovely to meet her on Sunday when the bell. Her lips was as white as snow and her neck was like a beechen bough. Young maidens went astray the river banks along. Girls that went to America were very brave. Ships was very dangerous in those days they was drove by sales. This peasant girl worked very hard to get money. After some years she felt lonely and got sick. Her friends were around her and she dying far from home. She told her friends to write a letter to her mother to meet her with God above. Her friends cut off a bit of her hair and sent it home in a letter and her love because she said to do it. She was buried in America because she withered far away. This is a sad song wrote in the time of Kickham to tell the people what a hard thing it is to die foreign. It makes weary hearts a cold and well night callous.

Paddy and Johnny reached fourteen in the same week, shortly after their final, and left joyfully to become citizens of the world together. The very next morning both came from the creamery by our windows, manfully smoking cigarettes and loftily surveying the shack as they passed, and Johnny sententiously observed to Paddy: 'God be wud the times *we* were in there.' After which we closed for the summer holidays in the grand consciousness of work well done.

From *Listen Here, Lads*!

FRANK WEBBER'S WAGER

By Charles Lever

I WAS SITTING at breakfast with Webber, when Power came in hastily.

'Ha, the very man!' said he. 'I say, O'Malley, here's an invitation for you from Sir George to dine on Friday. He desired me to say a thousand civil things about his not having made you out, regrets that he was not at home when you called yesterday, and all that.'

'By the way,' said Webber, 'wasn't Sir George Dashwood down in the West lately? Do you know what took him there?'

'Oh,' said Power, 'I can enlighten you. He got his wife west of the Shannon—a vulgar woman. She is now dead, and the only vestige of his unfortunate matrimonial connexion is a correspondence kept up with him by a maiden sister of his late wife's. She insists upon claiming the ties of kindred upon about twenty family eras during the year, when she regularly writes a most loving and ill-spelled epistle, containing the latest information from Mayo, with all particulars of the Macan family, of which she is a worthy member. To her constant hints of the acceptable nature of certain small remittances the poor General is never inattentive; but to the pleasing prospects of a visit in the flesh from Miss Judy Macan, the good man is dead.'

'Then, he has never yet seen her?'

'Never, and he hopes to leave Ireland without that blessing.'

'I say, Power, and has your worthy General sent me a card for his ball?'

'Not through me, Master Frank. Sir George must really be excused in this matter. He has a most attractive, lovely daughter, just at that budding, unsuspecting age when the heart

90

is most susceptible of impressions; and where, let me ask, could she run such a risk as in the chance of a casual meeting with the redoubted lady-killer, Master Frank Webber?'

'A very strong case, certainly,' said Frank; 'but still, had he confided his critical position to my honour and secrecy, he might have depended on me; now, having taken the other line, he must abide the consequences. I'll make fierce love to Lucy.'

'But how, may I ask, and when?'

'I'll begin at the ball, man.'

'Why, I thought you said you were not going?'

'There you mistake seriously. I merely said that I had not been invited.'

'Then, of course,' said I, 'Webber, you can't think of going, in any case, on my account.'

'My very dear friend, I go entirely upon my own. I not only shall go, but I intend to have most particular notice and attention paid me. I shall be prime favourite with Sir George —kiss Lucy—'

'Come, come! this is too strong.'

'What do you bet I don't? There, now, I'll give you a pony a-piece, I do. Do you say done?'

'That you kiss Miss Dashwood, and are not kicked downstairs for your pains; are those the terms of your wager?' inquired Power.

'With all my heart. That I kiss Miss Dashwood, and am not kicked downstairs for my pains.'

'Then I say, done!'

'And with you, too, O'Malley?'

'I thank you,' said I, coldly; 'I'm not disposed to make such a return for Sir George Dashwood's hospitality as to make an insult to his family the subject of a bet.'

'Why, man, what are you dreaming of? Miss Dashwood will not refuse my chaste salute. Come, Power, I will give you the other pony.'

'Agreed,' said he. 'At the same time, understand me distinctly —that I hold myself perfectly eligible to winning the wager by my own interference; for, if you do kiss her, I'll perform the remainder of the compact.'

'So I understand the agreement,' said Webber, and off he went.

I have often dressed for a storming party with less of trepidation than I felt on the evening of Sir George Dashwood's ball. It was long since I had seen Miss Dashwood; therefore, as to what precise position I might occupy in her favour was a matter of great doubt in my mind, and great import to my happiness.

Our quadrille over, I was about to conduct her to a seat, when Sir George came hurriedly up, his face greatly flushed, and betraying every semblance of high excitement.

'Read this,' said he, presenting a very dirty-looking note.

Miss Dashwood unfolded the billet, and after a moment's silence, burst out a-laughing, while she said, 'Why, really, papa, I do not see why this should put you out much, after all. Aunt may be somewhat of a character, as her note evinces; but after a few days——'

'Nonsense, child: there's nothing in this world I have such a dread of as this—and to come at such a time! O'Malley, my boy, read this note, and you will not feel surprised if I appear in the humour you see me.'

I read as follows:—

'Dear brother—When this reaches your hand I'll not be far off. I'm on my way up to town, to be under Dr. Dease for the ould complaint. Expect me to tea; and, with love to Lucy, believe me, yours in haste,

Judith Macan.

'Let the sheets be well aired in my room; and if you have a spare bed, perhaps you could prevail upon Father Magrath to stop, too.'

I scarcely could contain my laughter till I got to the end of this very free-and-easy epistle, when at last I burst forth in a hearty fit, in which I was joined by Miss Dashwood.

'I say, Lucy,' said Sir George, 'there's only one thing to be done. If this horrid woman does arrive, let her be shown to her room, and for the few days of her stay in town, we'll neither see nor be seen by anyone.'

Without waiting for a reply he was turning away, when the

servant announced, in his loudest voice, 'Miss Macan'.

No sooner had the servant pronounced the magical name than all the company present seemed to stand still. About two steps in advance of the servant was a tall, elderly lady, dressed in an antique brocade silk, with enormous flowers gaudily embroidered upon it. Her hair was powdered and turned back, in the fashion of fifty years before. Her short, skinny arms were bare, while on her hands she wore black silk mittens; a pair of green spectacles scarcely dimmed the lustre of a most piercing pair of eyes, to whose effect a very palpable touch of rouge on the cheeks certainly added brilliancy. There she stood, holding before her a fan about the size of a modern tea-tray, while at each repetition of her name by the servant she curtseyed deeply.

Sir George, armed with the courage of despair, forced his way through the crowd, and taking her hand affectionately, bid her welcome to Dublin. The fair Judy, at this, threw her arms about his neck, and saluted him with a hearty smack, that was heard all over the room.

'Where's Lucy, brother? Let me see my little darling,' said the lady, in a decided accent. 'There she is, I'm sure; kiss me, my honey.'

This office Miss Dashwood performed with an effort at courtesy really admirable; while, taking her aunt's arm, she led her to a sofa.

Power made his way towards Miss Dashwood, and succeeded in obtaining a formal introduction to Miss Macan.

'I hope you will do me the favour to dance next set with me, Miss Macan?'

'Really, Captain, it's very polite of you, but you must excuse me. I was never anything great in quadrilles: but if a reel or a jig——'

'Oh, dear aunt, don't think of it, I beg of you!'

'Or even Sir Roger de Coverley,' resumed Miss Macan.

'I assure you, quite equally impossible.'

'Then I'm certain you waltz,' said Power.

'What do you take me for, young man? I hope I know better. I wish Father Magrath heard you ask me that question; and for all your laced jacket——'

'Dearest aunt, Captain Power didn't mean to offend you; I'm certain he——'

'Well, why did he dare to—(sob, sob)—did he see anything light about me, that he—(sob, sob, sob)—oh, dear! oh, dear! is it for this I came up from my little peaceful place in the West?—(sob, sob, sob)—General, George, dear; Lucy, my love, I'm taken bad. Oh, dear! oh, dear! is there any whiskey negus?'

After a time she was comforted.

At supper later on in the evening, I was deep in thought when a dialogue quite near me aroused me from my reverie.

'Don't, now! don't, I tell ye; it's little ye know Galway, or ye wouldn't think to make up to me, squeezing my foot.'

'You're an angel, a regular angel. I never saw a woman suit my fancy before.'

'Oh, behave now. Father Magrath says——'

'Who's he?'

'The priest; no less.'

'Oh! bother him.'

'Bother Father Magrath, young man?'

'Well, then, Judy, don't be angry; I only means that a dragoon knows rather more of these matters than a priest.'

'Well, then, I'm not so sure of that. But, anyhow, I'd have you to remember it ain't a Widow Malone you have beside you.'

'Never heard of the lady,' said Power.

'Sure, it's a song—poor creature—it's a song they made about her in the North Cork when they were quartered down in our county.'

'I wish you'd sing it.'

'What will you give me, then, if I do?'

'Anything—everything—my heart—my life.'

'I wouldn't give a trauneen for all of them. Give me that old green ring on your finger, then.'

'It's yours,' said Power, placing it gracefully upon Miss Macan's finger; 'and now for your promise.'

'Well, mind you get up a good chorus, for the song has one, and here it is.'

'Miss Macan's song!' said Power, tapping the table with his knife.

'Miss Macan's song!' was re-echoed on all sides; and before the luckless General could interfere, she had begun:—

'Did ye hear of the Widow Malone,
                              Ohone!
Who lived in the town of Athlone,
                              Alone?
Oh! she melted the hearts
Of the swains in them parts,
 So lovely the widow Malone,
                              Ohone!
So lovely the Widow Malone.

'Of lovers she had a full score,
                              Or more;
And fortunes they all had galore,
                              In store;
From the Minister down
To the Clerk of the Crown,
All were courting the Widow Malone,
                              Ohone!
All were courting the Widow Malone.

'But so modest was Mrs. Malone,
                              'Twas known
No one ever could see her alone,
                              Ohone!
Let them ogle and sigh,
They could ne'er catch her eye,
So bashful the Widow Malone,
                              Ohone!
So bashful the Widow Malone.

'Till one Mr. O'Brien from Clare,—
                              How quare,
It's little for blushing they care,
                              Down there,

Put his arm round her waist,
Gave ten kisses, at laste,—
"Oh," says he, "you're my Molly Malone,"
              My own;
"Oh," says he, "you're my Molly Malone."

'And the widow they all thought so shy,
              My eye!
Ne'er thought of a simper or sigh;
              For why?
But "Lucius" says she,
"Since you've now made so free,
You may marry your Mary Malone,
              Ohone!
You may marry your Mary Malone."

'There's a moral contained in my song,
              Not wrong;
And, one comfort, it's not very long,
              But strong;
If for widows you die,
Larn to kiss, not to sigh,
For they're all like sweet Mistress Malone,
              Ohone!
Oh! they're very like Mistress Malone.'

Never did song create such a sensation as Miss Macan's.
'I insist upon a copy of "The Widow", Miss Macan,' said
Power.

'To be sure; give me a call tomorrow—let me see—about two.
Father Magrath won't be at home,' said she, with a coquettish
look.

'Where pray, may I pay my respects?'

Power produced a card and pencil, while Miss Macan wrote
a few lines, saying, as she handed it——

'There, now, don't read it here before all the people; they'll
think it mighty indelicate in me to make an appointment.'

Power pocketed the card, and the next minute Miss Macan's carriage was announced.

When she had taken her departure, 'Doubt it who will,' said Power, 'she has invited me to call on her tomorrow—written her address on my card—told me the hour she is certain of being alone. See here!' At these words he pulled forth the card, and handed it to a friend.

Scarcely were the eyes of the latter thrown upon the writing, when he said, 'So, this isn't it, Power!'

'To be sure it is, man. Read it out. Proclaim aloud my victory.'

Thus urged, his friend read:—

'Dear P.,—Please pay to my credit—and soon, mark ye—the two ponies lost this evening. I have done myself the pleasure of enjoying your ball, kissed the lady, quizzed the papa and walked into the cunning Fred Power.—Yours,
                                        Frank Webber.

'The Widow Malone, Ohone! is at your service.'

                                        From *Charles O'Malley*.

LADY BRACKNELL AND MR. WORTHING

By Oscar Wilde

LADY BRACKNELL. Mr. Worthing! Rise, sir, from this semi-recumbent posture. It is most indecorous.

GWENDOLEN. Mamma! [*He tries to rise: she restrains him*]. I must beg you to retire. This is no place for you. Besides, Mr. Worthing has not quite finished yet.

LADY BRACKNELL. Finished what, may I ask?

GWENDOLEN. I am engaged to Mr. Worthing, mamma. [*They rise together*].

LADY BRACKNELL. Pardon me, you are not engaged to any one. When you do become engaged to some one, I, or your father, should his health permit him, will inform you of the fact. An engagement should come on a young girl as a surprise, pleasant or unpleasant, as the case may be. It is hardly a matter that she could be allowed to arrange for herself. . . . And now I have a few questions to put to you, Mr. Worthing. While I am making these inquiries, you, Gwendolen, will wait for me below in the carriage.

GWENDOLEN. [*Reproachfully*]. Mamma!

LADY BRACKNELL. In the carriage, Gwendolen! [*Gwendolen goes to the door. She and Jack blow kisses to each other behind Lady Bracknell's back. Lady Bracknell looks vaguely about as if she could not understand what the noise was. Finally turns round*]. Gwendolen, the carriage!

GWENDOLEN. Yes, mamma. [*Goes out, looking back at Jack*].

LADY BRACKNELL. [*Sitting down.*] You can take a seat, Mr. Worthing. [*Looks in her pocket for notebook and pencil.*]

JACK. Thank you, Lady Bracknell, I prefer standing.

LADY BRACKNELL. [*Pencil and notebook in hand.*] I feel bound to tell you that you are not down on my list of eligible young men, although I have the same list as the dear Duchess of Bolton has. We work together in fact. However, I am quite ready to enter your name, should your answers be what a really affectionate mother requires. Do you smoke?

JACK. Well, yes, I must admit I smoke.

LADY BRACKNELL. I am glad to hear it. A man should always have an occupation of some kind. There are far too many idle men in London as it is. How old are you?

JACK. Twenty-nine.

LADY BRACKNELL. A very good age to be married at. I have always been of opinion that a man who desires to get married should know either everything or nothing. Which do you know?

JACK. [*After some hesitation.*] I know nothing, Lady Bracknell.

LADY BRACKNELL. I am pleased to hear it. I do not approve of anything that tampers with natural ignorance. Ignorance is like a delicate exotic fruit; touch it and the bloom is gone. The whole theory of modern education is radically unsound. Fortunately in England, at any rate, education produces no effect whatsoever. If it did, it would prove a serious danger to the upper classes, and probably lead to acts of violence in Grosvenor Square. What is your income?

JACK. Between seven and eight thousand a year.

LADY BRACKNELL. [*Makes a note in her book.*] In land, or in investments?

JACK. In investments, chiefly.

LADY BRACKNELL. That is satisfactory. What between the duties expected of one during one's lifetime, and the duties exacted from one after one's death, land has ceased to be either a profit or a pleasure. It gives one position, and prevents one from keeping it up. That's all that can be said about land.

JACK. I have a country house with some land, of course, attached to it, about fifteen hundred acres, I believe; but I don't depend on that for my real income. In fact, as far as I can make out, the poachers are the only people who make anything out of it.

LADY BRACKNELL. A country house! How many bedrooms? Well, that point can be cleared up afterwards. You have a town house, I hope? A girl with a simple, unspoiled nature, like Gwendolen, could hardly be expected to reside in the country.

JACK. I own a house in Belgrave Square, but it is let by the year to Lady Bloxham. Of course, I can get it back whenever I like, at six months' notice.

LADY BRACKNELL. Lady Bloxham? I don't know her.

JACK. Oh, she goes about very little. She is a lady considerably advanced in years.

LADY BRACKNELL. Ah, nowadays that is no guarantee of respectability of character. What number in Belgrave Square?

JACK. 149.

LADY BRACKNELL. [*Shaking her head.*] The unfashionable side. I thought there was something. However, that could easily be altered.

JACK. Do you mean the fashion, or the side?

LAYD BRACKNELL. [*Sternly*]. Both, if necessary, I presume. What are your politics?

JACK. I am afraid I really have none. I am a Liberal Unionist.

LADY BRACKNELL. Oh, they count as Tories. They dine with us. Or come in the evening, at any rate. Now to minor matters. Are your parents living?

JACK. I have lost both my parents.

LADY BRACKNELL. To lose one parent, Mr. Worthing, may be regarded as a misfortune; to lose both looks like carelessness. Who was your father? He was evidently a man of some wealth. Was he born in what the Radical papers call the purple of commerce, or did he rise from the ranks of the aristocracy?

JACK. I am afraid I really don't know. The fact is, Lady Bracknell, I said I had lost my parents. It would be nearer the truth to say that my parents seem to have lost me. . . I don't actually know who I am by birth. I was . . . well, I was found.

LADY BRACKNELL. Found!

JACK. The late Mr. Thomas Cardew, an old gentleman of a very charitable and kindly disposition, found me, and gave me the name of Worthing, because he happened to have a first-class ticket for Worthing in his pocket at the time. Worthing is a place in Sussex. It is a seaside resort.

LADY BRACKNELL. Where did the charitable gentleman who had

a first-class ticket for this seaside resort find you?

JACK. [*Gravely.*] In a hand-bag.

LADY BRACKNELL. A hand-bag?

JACK. [*Very seriously.*] Yes, Lady Bracknell. I was in a hand-bag —a somewhat large, black leather hand-bag, with handles to it—an ordinary hand-bag in fact.

LADY BRACKNELL. In what locality did this Mr. James, or Thomas, Cardew come across this ordinary hand-bag?

JACK. In the cloakroom at Victoria Station. It was given to him in mistake for his own.

LADY BRACKNELL. The cloak-room at Victoria Station?

JACK. Yes. The Brighton line.

LADY BRACKNELL. The line is immaterial. Mr. Worthing, I confess I feel somewhat bewildered by what you have just told me. To be born, or at any rate bred, in a hand-bag, whether it had handles or not, seems to me to display a contempt for the ordinary decencies of family life that reminds one of the worst excesses of the French Revolution. And I presume you know what that unfortunate movement led to? As for the particular locality in which the hand-bag was found, a cloak-room at a railway station might serve to conceal a social indiscretion—has probably, indeed, been used for that purpose before now—but it could hardly be regarded as an assured basis for a recognized position in good society.

JACK. May I ask you then what you would advise me to do? I need hardly say I would do anything in the world to ensure Gwendolen's happiness.

LADY BRACKNELL. I would strongly advise, Mr. Worthing, to try and acquire some relations as soon as possible, and to make a definite effort to produce at any rate one parent, of either sex, before the season is quite over.

JACK. Well, I don't see how I could possibly manage to do that. I can produce the hand-bag at any moment. It is in my dressing-room at home. I really think that should satisfy you, Lady Bracknell.

LADY BRACKNELL. Me, sir! What has it to do with me? You can hardly imagine that I and Lord Bracknell would dream of allowing our only daughter—a girl brought up with the utmost care—to marry into a cloak-room, and form an alliance with a parcel! Good morning, Mr. Worthing!

[*Lady Bracknell sweeps out in majestic indignation.*]

JACK. Good morning! [*Algernon, from the other room, strikes up the Wedding March. Jack looks perfectly furious, and goes to the door.*] For goodness' sake don't play that ghastly tune, Algy! How idiotic you are!

[*The music stops and Algernon enters cheerily.*]

ALGERNON. Didn't it go off all right, old boy? You don't mean to say Gwendolen refused you? I know it is a way she has. She is always refusing people. I think it is most ill-natured of her.

JACK. Oh, Gwendolen is as right as a trivet. As far as she is concerned, we are engaged. Her mother is perfectly unbearable. Never met such a Gorgon . . . I don't really know what a Gorgon is like, but I am quite sure that Lady Bracknell is one. In any case, she is a monster, without being a myth, which is rather unfair. . . . I beg your pardon, Algy, I suppose I shouldn't talk about your own aunt in that way before you.

ALGERNON. My dear boy, I love hearing my relations abused. It is the only thing that makes me put up with them at all. Relations are simply a tedious pack of people, who haven't got the remotest knowledge of how to live, nor the smallest instinct about when to die.

JACK. Oh, that is nonsense!

ALGERNON. It isn't!

JACK. Well, I won't argue about the matter. You always want to argue about things.

ALGERNON. That is exactly what things were originally made for.

JACK. Upon my word, if I thought that, I'd shoot myself. . . . [*A pause.*] You don't think there is any chance of Gwendolen becoming like her mother in about a hundred and fifty years, do you, Algy?

ALGERNON. All women become like their mothers. That is their tragedy. No man does. That's his.

From *The Importance of Being Earnest*

LET WELL ALONE

By Lennox Robinson

A Little Moral Farce in One Act.

Characters:
JUDY RODDY.
MRS. RODDY, HER MOTHER.
ANDY FINNEGAN.
SERGEANT GOGGIN.
GUARD MICHAEL DEVINE.
PATIENCE TYNDALL.
HILDA, HER SISTER.
TIMOTHY TUMULTY.

The scene is a mountainy road, wild and rocky. There is heather and autumn furze. In the centre, or perhaps to one side, some ruined masonry which might be the remains of an old mine-shaft or a well. It sticks up above the stage for three or four feet.

A girl of twelve or thirteen, JUDY RODDY, *is sitting on a big stone, crying at the top of her lungs. An elderly labouring man,* ANDY FINNEGAN, *comes in.*

ANDY. Gracious sake, Judy Roddy, what ails you? [*Judy cries a bit louder.*] Is it sick you are or is someone after dying?

JUDY. [*Between her sobs.*] Me lamb, me little lamb.

ANDY. Your what?

JUDY. Me lamb, me little Cornelius; dead and drowned.

ANDY. Your dear, little orphan lamb, the pet of the village?

JUDY. [*Nodding.*] I had him in me arms, showing him the dark water and he slipped from me grasp. . . . I can hear him bleating—he's alive yet.

103

ANDY. Alive, where?

JUDY. In the well. [*Hysterically.*] Fetch the guards, fetch the guards.

ANDY. That's a terrible thing. [*Looking down the well.*] I don't think I see him.

JUDY. [*Joining him.*] Over there in the far corner, it's like as if he had lepped on a rock.

ANDY. I think I can make him out—no, I can't.

JUDY. Ah, Andy, me heart's broken. [*Calling down the well.*] Baa, Baa! Keep your courage up, sure aren't the guards only round the corner of the road. Run, Andy, and fetch them, Hurry.

ANDY. I will so. [*As he hurries out he meets Mrs. Roddy.*]

MRS. RODDY. What's the pillalouing about?

ANDY. The child dropped her lamb. [*He disappears.*]

MRS. RODDY. She what? What's on you Judy?

JUDY. [*A little more composed.*] I know I'm to blame, Mammy, but don't ask me how it happened . . . [*calling down the well.*] Have a bit of spunk, Corney, darling, help's not far off. Baa, baa! I see the Sergeant and dear Michaeleen Devine mounting the hill.

MRS. RODDY. [*Peering down the well.*] Glory be to goodness. Is it there poor little Cornelius is?

JUDY. Don't you see him? Stuck on the cold rocks.

MRS. RODDY. I do. . . . I think.

JUDY. I that nursed him from the day he was born an orphan, teaspoonfuls of milk, sugar and the best of grass, and to look at him now [*noise of voices*]—Oh, thank God, here's the guards.

    [*Sergeant Goggin and a young guard, Michael Devine, come in, followed by Andy.*]

SERGEANT. This is a queer, bad business.

MRS. RODDY. 'Tis terrible. The poor child's in a fit over it.

SERGEANT. Tch, tch, tch. [*He looks down the well.*]

JUDY. Do you see it? There on the far side, pressed up against the rocks.

SERGEANT. I do to be sure. Do you think I'm blind?

JUDY. Won't one of yous—you Michaeleen—climb down and bring it back to me, me poor little motherless lamb?

SERGEANT. Faith, 'twould be no joke to go climbing down there. How far down is it, Michael?

MICHAEL. I couldn't say, Sergeant.

SERGEANT. And no knowing the depth of water in the well.

MICHAEL. 'Tisn't a well at all, only a shaft that was for the copper-mine in the long-ago times.

SERGEANT. 'Twasn't a copper-mine, 'twas a gold-mine. Sure in the ancient times wasn't Ireland rotten with gold?

MICHAEL. Lead.

SERGEANT. There was never copper in Ireland.

JUDY. [*Breaking out afresh.*] Oh, let you stop talking of copper and gold and lead and me lamb drowning. Have you no heart? I'll climb down after him meself.

SERGEANT. [*Stopping her.*] You'll do no such thing.

JUDY. [*Running to Michael.*] Oh, Michaeleen, dear, darling, Michaeleen, let you go down and fetch me lamb for me.

MRS. RODDY. Yes, do Michaeleen. Like a good boy.

ANDY. Over with you, Michael.

MICHAEL. How smart you are with your 'good boys' and your 'over with yous'. Is it to drown me yes want?

SERGEANT. A wonderful chance that's come your way.

ANDY. I've a suguan behind the hedge, I made it for tying the rick of hay, I'll have it for you in a jiffy. [*He hurries out.*] We'll tie it round you instead.

SERGEANT. Good. So you'll be in no danger at all.

MRS. RODDY. Gorgeous! The sort of thing would get you a medal.

MICHAEL. I don't want no bloody medal.

JUDY. Me lamb, me lamb!

SERGEANT. Well, maybe you'd get a Carnegie watch. And you'll be in no danger, for don't we all know the fine swimmer you are, first in the August regatta, but for the sake of getting the watch we'll let on you can't swim a stroke.

MICHAEL. And for the sake of a gold watch that maybe won't go, am I to go paddling round and round like a goldfish in muck and slime and eels and—and everything?

ANDY. [*Back with the suguan.*] Here I am, Sergeant. We'll make a twist of it round his waist.

MICHAEL. You won't then. 'Tis a dirty old rope which would have me new tunic destroyed.

SERGEANT. Be the hokey, I forgot about the clothes. Apart from the rope, it's likely the side of the well is all dirt and slime.

MICHAEL. Of course it is.

SERGEANT. You'd better strip.

MICHAEL. I 'ont.

SERGEANT. I'll get into trouble with the authorities if I let you destroy your new tunic.

JUDY. Me little lamb!

SERGEANT. Off with it, them's me orders to you.

MICHAEL. I suppose I must, so. [*To Judy.*] You and your blasted lamb. [*Judy cries.*]

MRS. RODDY. Oh, such a thing to say to the innocent child! For shame, Michaeleen Devine.

SERGEANT. Strip yourself now, we're losing time arguing, and the poor little creature stifling in the water. [*They all help him out of his tunic which Judy folds and lays out of sight behind the well.*]. I wonder what about the trousers?

MICHAEL. I'll take off no trousers. You can order me till you're black in the face.

MRS. RODDY. Sure we're all friends here.

MICHAEL. I think 'tis innimies ye are. Anyway, friends or innimies, I'll stick to me pants.

SERGEANT. O.K. Hand me the rope, Andy. [*They tie the rope round his waist and are making for the well-head.*] Oh, we should arrange some signals like. Would we say one tug to let him down and two to draw him up?

MRS. RODDY. I think two to let him down would be nicer, 'tis more usual, like the two claps of a bell on a bus.

SERGEANT. Whatever you say, ma'am, is all right with me. Do you understand the signals, Michael?

MICHAEL. [*They have him at the edge of the well.*] I think I do. Whatever you do, for the love of Mike, keep a strong hoult

on the bloody rope. [*As he goes over the top.*] Oh, oh, blessed
Saint Christopher, preserver of all who are in danger—[*he
disappears.*]

[*Miss Patience and Miss Hilda Tyndall come in. They
are in the sixties, tweedily and Protestantly dressed.*]

PATIENCE. We'll just walk to the top of the hill, Hilda, and
come back by the bog road.

HILDA. Whatever you like, Patience. Oh, what's going on here?

SERGEANT. The Guard's down the well, Miss Tyndall.

PATIENCE. The Guard?

HILDA. The old R.I.C. dear, only different—but I'm told
quite as respectable.

PATIENCE. Nonsense. I don't believe it.

SERGEANT. It's a fact, miss. He is down the well.

PATIENCE. I didn't mean that, I meant respectability.

MRS. RODDY. And the lamb, Miss Patience——

JUDY. Oh, oh, oh. Me little Cornelius.

MRS. RODDY. Shut your mouth, child. I'm sorry, miss, but
we're in a speck of trouble here.

SERGEANT. You see, it's like this—[*a chuck on the rope he is
holding almost pulls him over.*] He wants to come up. Haul
away, Andy. You'll have your lamb in two ticks, Judy.
God, you wouldn't think there was so much weight in that
fellow. Would you oblige by lending a hand, ladies, there's
a life at stake.

PATIENCE. Of course. A life at stake! Hilda! Mrs. Roddy!
[*They all seize the rope.*] I remember after the choir festival
there always used to be sports at the Rectory and the tug-of-war
was such fun.

[*They pull strenuously. Michael appears, he is only visible
to his waist. His shirt is rather dirty: so is his face.*]

SERGEANT. Have you the lamb?

MICAHEL. I haven't, but I've——

SERGEANT, MRS. RODDY. You haven't?

JUDY. Me little Corney!

MICHAEL. I've something different.

SERGEANT. What?

MICHAEL. This. [*He discloses a piece of wet sacking with some-thing inside it.*]

SERGEANT. What's that?

MICHAEL. I dunno. But it's something.

SERGEANT. And how deep is the well, and what class of a well is it?

MICHAEL. Not so deep, I'm only wet up to the knees so there's no need to be swimming, but there's a power of queer things in that same well. There's a box, a sort of lawyer's box stuck in the wall half-way down——

PATIENCE. Oh!

HILDA. Are you ill, dear?

PATIENCE. Of course not.

MICHAEL. Let ye open the bag.

ANDY. Ay. [*He and the Sergeant open the bag.*] Bones, be dad, a pile of old bones.

MRS. RODDY. I'd say, they'd be a pile of old cows' bones.

SERGEANT. Do you remember the time Timothy Tumulty was in danger of getting into trouble with us on the head of selling rotten meat?

MRS. RODDY. I do, of course. Why didn't yes convict him?

SERGEANT. We couldn't lay hands on the meat.

PATIENCE. [*To her sister.*] The girl at the lodge—I know she had a baby.

HILDA. The gardener?

PATIENCE. No, dear, the gardener's boy.

HILDA. Oh, I never understood—

PATIENCE. You were too young.

MRS. RODDY. She's a brazen piece, that one at the lodge. You'd de well to hunt her.

[*Timothy Tumulty comes in. A heavy man*].

SERGEANT. Oh, Mr. Tumulty, queer you should happen along just now. Where have you been?

TIMOTHY. Minding my business. Just buying a cow up the mountains that yous might all have a nice Sunday dinner.

SERGEANT. Was she a very sick cow?

TIMOTHY. I don't know what you mean, or if I do I deeply resent that remark.

SERGEANT. We've been fishing in the well.

MRS. RODDY. And finding a strange, a very strange thing.

TIMOTHY. It's a wonder you wouldn't find something better to do.

MICHAEL. Good-bye all. Keep a good hoult of the rope. [*He disappears.*].

TIMOTHY. What's the meaning of all this?

PATIENCE. [*Pointing to the sacking and the bones.*] What's the meaning of that?

MRS. RODDY. Ay, explain them away if you can, Timothy Tumulty.

ANDY. Ah, quiet yourself, Mrs. Roddy. Let things rest.

HILDA. There should be coroners, there should be a state pathologist, people should be confronted with the remains.

PATIENCE. Yes. Doesn't a murderer burst out bleeding?

TIMOTHY. What murderer are you talking about?

SERGEANT. We haven't got as far as murder yet.

MRS. RODDY. It may be only a question of rotten meat—which might make trouble for some people.

TIMOTHY. I don't like that look you gave me, Mrs. Roddy.

MRS. RODDY. I'll look the way I please, Timothy Tumulty.

SERGEANT. There's a few questions I'd like to put to you— [*He is chucked again.*] Oh, here's Michael back. Lend a hand, Timothy.

TIMOTHY. I'll take no act or part in this, [*The others all haul.*]

JUDY. Well, I hope he brings me little Cornelius this time. [*Michael appears, he is much dirtier, he has a black tin box in his hand.*]

MICHAEL. 'Tis the box I was talking about, stuck in the wall, as dry as a pea and it came open in me hand.

SERGEANT. [*Taking it from him.*] There's printing on it. [*Reading it with difficulty.*] Major Robert Tyndall, D.S.O.

HILDA. Father's box! Many a time I've seen it. Patience, you remember how we missed it after he died. The lawyer said his will was in it. How extraordinary.

PATIENCE. Give me that box.

HILDA. No, let me see. [*She gets it from the Sergeant.*]

PATIENCE. I forbid you to open it.

HILDA. I've as much right as you have—[*they struggle for the box but Hilda wins and opens it and takes out a document.*] Oh, it is the will. 'Last will and testament—'

PATIENCE. [*With a moan.*] The bureau!

HILDA. What bureau?

PATIENCE. The lovely Sheraton one in the library.

HILDA. That shabby old thing?

SERGEANT. [*Getting an awful chuck.*] God! Excuse me, ladies. Michaeleen's gone again. [*He has.*]

TIMOTHY. I'm not going to let this thing rest where it is. There's insinuations being made against me and me meat.

ANDY. Sure it may only be the baby from the lodge.

MRS. RODDY. I'd arrest him on suspicion, Sergeant.

TIMOTHY. Suspicion? There was no suspicion about the endorsement on your licence.

MRS. RODDY. Oh, such a thing to drag up!

TIMOTHY. Endorsed twice.

MRS. RODDY. Funerals each time. A little drop of comfort for the mourners.

HILDA. I must know the truth. What's in the will?

PATIENCE. No different from the other ones, everything divided between us, only you were to get the bureau.

ANDY. What's a bureau?

MRS. RODDY. An old chest of drawers.

ANDY. Oh, fighting about a couple of old drawers.

PATIENCE. It's nothing to you, Hilda, you don't care about that sort of thing but I do, and when I saw in his last will —he was always making wills—that he had left you the beautiful bureau—I couldn't bear it—I—I—

HILDA. When did you steal the box?

PATIENCE. The morning before he died. I went and taught Sunday-school afterwards. It wasn't exactly stealing—

SERGEANT. Here, what's this talk of stealing?

HILDA. [*With dignity.*] I shouldn't have used the word, Sergeant, there could be no question of stealing between my sister and myself. But I think there are very queer things being fished out of this well, certain reputations will be a little smirched by the time that well is emptied. Mr. Tumulty, the girl at our lodge, Mrs. Roddy——

MICHAEL. [*Appearing dirtier than ever.*] I'm back. I didn't go far this time. Look what I have for you, Sergeant. [*He exhibits a small box.*]

SERGEANT. What's this?

MICHAEL. Don't you recognise it? It's the ballot-box was missing at the last election.

SERGEANT. Holy O! So it is.

MICHAEL. I forget now was it the F.F.s or the F.G.s kidnapped it. I know 'twas suspected that if it had been opened there'd be a big difference in the result. I'm going down again. Talk of pearl-fishers——! [*He disappears.*]

SERGEANT. Stop. Come back. [*But he is gone.*]. I wonder should I count the votes. The box is locked.

ANDY. Yerra, let it lie. What the hell difference if it was an F.F. or a F.G. got the place.

[*The Sergeant turns over the box, a stream of water comes out of the slit.*]

SERGEANT. I'm afeard they're melted.

ANDY. Thank God.

MRS. RODDY. And all this time no trace of Judy's lamb.

SERGEANT. Yes, indeed. We're getting everything except the bloody lamb.

JUDY. [*Crying and bawling down the well.*] Baa, baa!

SERGEANT. Hi, Michael. What about the lamb? [*A distant mumble from Michael.*]

ANDY. Rotten old bones and quarrelling and abuse and no sign of the little lamb. Give me back me rope and let me away out of this.

SERGEANT. [*Having being chucked.*] Whisht! Here's Michael again. Maybe he has the lamb this time.

MICHAEL. [*Dirtier than ever, he speaks in a voice of tragedy.*] It's awful.

EVERYONE. What is?

MICHAEL. A drowned Garda. Look! [*He comes out of the well, he is wet to the knees, his boots a mass of mud, he holds up a wet, muddy tunic.*]

SERGEANT. What's that?

MICHAEL. A tunic. A drowned Garda's tunic. [*He stifles a sob. Timothy reverently raises his hat.*]

SERGEANT. The poor, decent man. How at all did he get there?

MICHAEL. That will likely never be known.

MRS. RODDY. It'll be the lad that disappeared three years ago. They said America, but I had my suspicions.

PATIENCE. How do you know he's drowned, Sergeant?

SERGEANT. Look at the tunic, Miss.

PATIENCE. Nonsense. If he was drowned wouldn't he be inside the tunic?

SERGEANT. That's true, I suppose, but in the best cases of drowning the clothes are always left on the beach. Whose tunic would it be, I wonder? There's not so many Gardai hereabouts. There's may be some identification marks in the pockets. I'll have a look. [*He starts to look.*]

JUDY. [*Very sympathetic.*] Are you cold, Michaeleen?

MICHAEL. I am, Judy.

JUDY. And all mud and slime.

MICHAEL. Yes.

JUDY. And your pants—a fright.

MICHAEL. I know.

JUDY. And your boots—worse again?

MICHAEL. They are.

JUDY. In short, you're a sight. A kind of scare-crow would be stuck in a field to keep the birdeens from the seed-oats.

MICHAEL. I suppose so.

JUDY. I was thinking so meself. [*She laughs.*]

SERGEANT. There's no evidence in the pockets except a plain sodden handkerchief, a packet of Woodbines and a bookie's ticket.

MICHAEL. That's not much to go on.

SERGEANT. Oh, we could trace him through the bookie.

PATIENCE. You see, Hilda, the Guards are betters—I mean, they bet. The old R.I.C. never——

TIMOTHY. [*Reading the ticket over the Sergeant's shoulder*]. Jeremiah Molloy, Casement Street.

MICHAEL. Oh, he was betting with Jerry, was he? The poor fella.

SERGEANT. And on the back of it written in pencil—'tis nearly washed away—'Fairy Queen' a shilling each way.

MICHAEL. Here. Hold on. Let me see that ticket. [*He snatches it from the Sergeant, it is so damp that it tears.*]

SERGEANT. Damn it, you're destroying the evidence.

MICHAEL. It's me writing, it's me ticket, it's me handkerchief, me initials are on it, Auntie Floss gave me a present of six for the Christmas—it's me new tunic.

[*Consternation.*]

SERGEANT. But didn't I help you off with your tunic not ten minutes ago, and didn't Judy fold it up and put it behind the well?

ANDY. She did. I saw her do it myself.

SERGEANT. And are you at the betting and the gambling again? Don't you know I've set me face against it? [*Judy laughs, a silvery laugh.*] Ah, Judy, with all the clatteration, we're forgetting your little lamb.

[*A baa is heard. They all rush to the well except Judy, who runs out on the other side.*]

CHORUS. The creature. I heard it. Down there. That side. No, this side. Stuck to the rocks. Its feet in a puddle. [*A louder baa.*] Sergeant! Michaeleen! Patience! Hilda! Andy! Mrs. Roddy! Timothy Tumulty!

JUDY. [*Coming back, a young lamb in her arms*]. Doaty little Cornelius.

SERGEANT. Cornelius? How did you get him out?

JUDY. [*Innocently.*] Out? Out of where?

SERGEANT. The well, of course.

JUDY. Sure he never was in no well. To think I'd let little Corny drop down a well!

SERGEANT. But what's the lamb in the well, so?

JUDY. There's no lamb in the well.

MRS. RODDY. But you showed him to me.

ANDY. And to me.

PATIENCE. Didn't you see it, Hilda?

HILDA. I—I—

SERGEANT. Didn't you see it, Michael?

MICHAEL. I did not. Did you see it yourself?

JUDY. Ah, you all let on to be seeing it for fear you'd be counted blind.

MICHAEL. But, Judy, why on earth—?

JUDY. [*Laughing again.*] Ah, Michaeleen, you were very rude to me. You said I was a bold child and an ugly child and that I deserved a slapping and you gave me a slap on me behind. So I vowed I'd pay you out. And look at you now —the cut of you! And 'tis I threw your new tunic down the well when you were arguing about the rope, and 'tis your boots trampled it into the mud and the water, and I hope the ticket for races is melted on you or that your old horse never gets beyond the first lap.

MICHAEL. You limb of the devil.

SERGEANT. That child's born to tread the gallows.

MRS. RODDY. Oh, Judy, you bold brat.

ANDY. The harrum she's done. It's been said before—truth at the bottom of a well. Let it lie there, says I.

JUDY. Good-bye, Michael. Maybe ye'll be more respectful to me in future. Darling little Cornelius. [*And she goes out with the lamb.*]

MICHAEL. Blast her! Anyhow, as I am a sight, to hell with it and I'll go down fishing again. [*He starts for the well.*]

ANDY. Stop. Let ye all stop. There's maybe things at the bottom of that well are better left there.

SERGEANT. I want to know the truth.

ANDY. Ay, truth and the like. We've been getting truth the day and much good has it done us—and we don't know if it is the truth. Only the Lord Almighty on the Day of Judgment will be able to tell us about them bones; all the lawyers in Ireland won't be able to count and recount these voting papers; and look at the harrum the finding of the old Colonel's will has made—two sisters sparring that never had a cross

word for each other before. Miss Patience and Miss Hilda,
let ye make it up and be friends.

HILDA. Why didn't you ask me for the bureau, Patience?
I'm sure I never wanted the old thing. I'd far rather have
something smart and new.

PATIENCE. Then, I can take it out of the library and have it
in my own little room?

ANDY. [*Taking the box.*] There goes the old will, bad cess to it
[*drops it down the well*]. And, Sergeant, won't you send the
ballot-box to follow it?

SERGEANT. I don't think such a thing would be within me rights.

ANDY. Ah, your rights! There's many a thing you do worse
than that. Drop it down, and the bag of bones along with it.

SERGEANT. Very well. [*As he is doing so, Judy comes in with
the lamb.*]

JUDY. What are you doing?

SERGEANT. Stand back, Judy. Harm enough you've done already
today.

JUDY. I must see. [*She climbs on the edge of the well, and as
the last object is dropped, the lamb slips over too.*]

JUDY. Oh, me lamb, me little lamb!

SERGEANT. Be the hokey, it's gone this time, in earnest. Over
with you, Michael.

MICHAEL. I 'on't.

PATIENCE. For shame. The poor little child's lamb.

SERGEANT. Let yes all lend a hand to put him over.

    [*Michael protests, but they surround him and as they
    are lowering him the curtain falls.*]

From *The Bell.*

THE PRIESTIN' OF FATHER JOHN

By John D. Sheridan

They'll be priestin' him the morra—
Troth it's a quare world too!
For I min' the rascal that he was,
And the things he used to do.
Many's the time I chased him
When the strawberries were ripe
Though I own I never caught him—
He was faster nor a snipe.
He hit me wi' a snowball once,
And that same very hand
Will be blessin' me the morra—
Troth it's hard to understand.

Long Richard from Kircubbin,
Who's a sort of far-out frien',
Is strutting' round this fortnight back,
Just like a hatchin' hen.
McAllister from Cargey,
Who's no more to him nor me,
You'd think to hear the chat of him
He reared him on his knee.
Tom the Tailor's nearly bet
From hurryin' on new suits,
And there's powerful heavy buyin'
On caps and yella boots.
The Square is thick wi' buntin'—
Man dear there'll be a sight
When the late bus from Downpatrick
Gets in the morra night.

116

Ool' Canon Dan, God bless him,
Will be fussin' fit to burst,
And the women batin' other
To get the blessin' first.
But, Canon or no Canon,
And I'd say this till his face,
For all his bit o' purple
He'll take the second place.
Sure even if the Bishop came
Wi' yon big mitre on
He wouldn't get the welcome
That we'll give to Father John.

The pains are at me constant now,
I seldom cross the door—
But I'm crossin' it the morra
If I never cross it more.
You can quit your scoldin', Julia,
An' sayin' I'm not wise—
Sure the sight of him will ease me heart
An' gladden me oul' eyes.
It won't be easy bendin',
An' the oul' knees will hurt,
But I'll get down there fornenst him
In all the mud and dirt.

And if I get a chance at all
I'll whisper in his ear
[Och I'll do it nice and quiet
So that no one else will hear]:
'If anything should happen me
Before you go away,
It's no one but yourself I want
To shrive me for the clay.
Th' oul' Canon mightn't like it,
For he's still hale and strong,
And I'm sure if he anointed me

He wouldn't do it wrong.
But I'd feel more contented
If the hand that helped me go
Was the hand that threw the snowball
Twenty years ago.'

From *Joe's no Saint*.